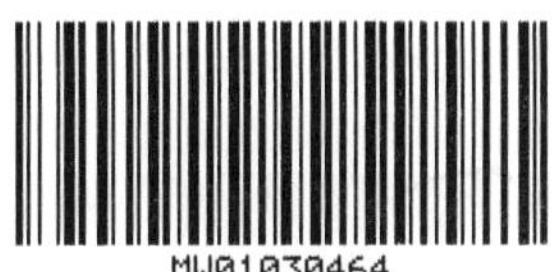

The Greatest Commandment

Also by Fulton J. Sheen
from Sophia Institute Press:

Victory over Vice

Archbishop Sheen's Book of Sacraments

Fulton Sheen's Wartime Prayer Book

God's World and Our Place in It

The Cries of Jesus from the Cross

Lord, Teach Us to Pray

Archbishop Fulton J. Sheen

The Greatest Commandment

A Fulton Sheen Anthology on Love

Edited by Al Smith

SOPHIA INSTITUTE PRESS
Manchester, New Hampshire

Cover design by LUCAS Art & Design, Jenison, MI.

On the cover: *Washing of the Feet* (1591–1592), by Palma il Giovane, Wikimedia Commons, public domain.

Scripture translations are taken from the Douay-Rheims edition of the Bible.

Sophia Institute Press
Box 5284, Manchester, NH 03108
1-800-888-9344

www.SophiaInstitute.com

paperback ISBN 978-1-64413-564-8

ebook ISBN 978-1-64413-565-5

Library of Congress Control Number: 2021948453

First printing

To
Mary, gracious mother
of the Divine Christ,
who promised not to make
us servants but friends

This is my commandment,
that you love one another,
as I have loved you.

—John 15:12

Contents

The Best of Fulton J. Sheen: God Love You

Introduction

Archbishop Fulton J. Sheen was a man for all seasons. Over his lifetime, he spent himself for souls, transforming lives with the clear teaching of the truths of Christ and His Church through his books, radio addresses, lectures, television series, and his many newspaper columns.

As a much sought-after lecturer, his topics ranged from the social concerns of the day to matters of faith and morals. With an easy and personable manner, Sheen could strike up a conversation on just about any subject, making numerous friends as well as converts.

During his presentations, Archbishop Sheen would offer his trademark words of benediction, "God love you." Sheen explained that this phrase "God love you" means God is love, God loves you, and you ought to love God in return.

Along with his familiar parting phrase of "God love you," Archbishop Sheen was known for beginning his lectures with the greeting "Friends." This salutation had a twofold meaning: he was referring to the Scripture passage "I will not now call you servants ... but I have called you friends" (John 15:15). And, he wanted to make friends with men and women of all faiths, in the hope of gradually helping them to come to know the Lord Jesus Christ.

With love as its central focus, this anthology begins with a collection of essays and prayers compiled by Fulton Sheen under the title *Love One Another*, published by P. J. Kenedy and Sons, New York, in 1944. In these writings, Sheen speaks to Catholics, Protestants, and Jews regarding the fostering of friendships between various religious groups. Additionally, he makes several practical suggestions on how to improve relations between people of varying backgrounds. An array of reflections is presented for devotional inspiration, simultaneously laying out a groundwork in spiritual values proven to facilitate harmonious relationships.

There are some who have considered this work a must-read for those sincerely interested in seeking the attainment of a genuine brotherhood of man. Others may find in this collection some prayerful and practical solutions to many of today's most challenging interpersonal problems. Archbishop Fulton Sheen made it clear that the command given by Jesus to "love thy neighbour as thyself" (Mark 12:31) is clearly an effective answer to combating the sin of intolerance.

The second part of this anthology contains a collection of thought-provoking writings compiled by Sheen into a book originally titled, *The Best of Fulton J. Sheen—God Love You*, published by the Maco Magazine Corporation, New York, in 1955. Each paragraph has been selected from over two dozen books written by him for the particular help and guidance they can bring to the reader. These brief, incisive selections from Archbishop Sheen reveal the mind of a brilliant man and a true pastor of souls.

In this anthology, you will find a treasury of guideposts wherein Sheen highlights the role of the virtues, the passions, and the value of personal introspection. He engages the reader using his unique blend of sensitivity and humor.

During one of his radio addresses in 1944, Archbishop Sheen fondly said, "I have always addressed you as friends, and you know that unseen friends are sometimes the best friends. To say 'my friends,' would be to claim a privilege. But friends are the expression of a hope. A hope that by listening to me, I may with traitorous trueness and with loyal deceit, betray you into the hands of the God of Love and Mercy."

Friends, "a new commandment I give unto you: That you love one another, as I have loved you, that you also love one another. By this shall all men know that you are my disciples, if you have love one for another" (John 13:34–35).

Love One Another

✠

I have called you friends. . . .
A new commandment I give unto you:
That you love one another, as I have loved you.

—John 15:15; 13:34

1

The Foundation of Love—God

"Man came from the beast; therefore he ought to love his fellowman."

How silly that sounds! Everyone knows that the law of the survival of the fittest can never evolve into love, nor can the struggle for existence develop into human brotherhood. If we come from the beasts, then we may appropriately be expected to act like beasts.

Start with another philosophy of life, that love originates in Heaven. "A new commandment I give unto you, that you love one another; that as I have loved you, you also love one another. By this will all men know that you are my disciples, if you have love for one another" (John 13:34–35).

Loving one another is now reasonable, because the God of love made us, because the God of love redeemed us, and because the God of love sanctified us.

What Does It Mean to Say That God Is Love?

Love is (a) mutual self-giving, (b) which ends in self-realization. Love first of all involves reciprocity and "otherness." A love that cannot diffuse itself is not love for love raised to its highest power is a mutual self-giving.

All love, therefore, implies generation: the giving not of what one has, but of what one is.

Perfect love is an *Act*. Sterile, selfish love is the negation of love. A love that refuses to propagate itself is not love. Goodness is necessarily social.

Secondly, perfect love is not merely mutual self-giving; otherwise, it might end in exhaustion. There must, therefore, be added to the idea of giving that of self-recovery.

In addition to the Source that gives and the Stream that flows from it, there must be the Sea in which all is recovered without loss, and without cessation.

Raised to the infinite, the Love that generates is the Father; the Love that is generated from all eternity is the Son. That such Love would there end would be less than loving. Love must circle back upon itself, and that eternal bond of love uniting Father and Son is called the Holy Spirit.

To put it in other words, I can know something of the existence of God, something of His Infinite Power, Life, and Beauty by contemplating His universe, but I could never divine anything of His secret Thought and Love unless He told me. His creation gives but dim hints of these.

It was, therefore, only natural that man should desire further knowledge of the inner life of God and, in seeking that light, would ask such questions as Plato asked four centuries before Christ:

> "If there is only one God, what does He think about? If He is an intelligent being, He must think of something.
>
> "If there is only one God, whom does He love? for to be happy one must love."

These questions were hurled against the high heavens as so much brass, for there was no man to give them an answer. The answer could come only from God Himself, and it came when Our Blessed Lord appeared on earth and revealed to us the inmost life of God, namely, there are three Persons in God, God the Father, God the Son, and God the Holy Ghost. This tremendous mystery is known as the Trinity.

If we would answer the questions of Plato and know what God thinks about, and whom God loves, let us first ask the questions of man, for man has been made to the image and likeness of God. The study of man's thought and man's will should tell us something about the Thought and the Will of God.

Of the thought of man, three things may be said, namely: It is a word; it is generated or born; and it is personal.

Man thinks; he thinks a thought, such as "Justice," "Faith," "Fortitude," or "Charity." Now, these thoughts are words; they are words even before I speak them, for the vocal word is only the expression of the internal word in my mind.

These thoughts or internal words are generated or born. Who, for example, ever sat down to a meal with "Justice"? Who ever heard of "Charity" going out for a walk? Who knows the size, the weight, and the color of "Fortitude"?

No one has ever seen, tasted, or touched these thoughts, and yet they are real. They are spiritual thoughts.

But where did they come from? Since they are not wholly in the outside world, they must have been produced, or generated, by the mind itself; not with that physical birth by which animal produces animal, but by a spiritual generation by which we produce ideas or internal words.

There are other ways of begetting life, we must remember, than physically. The most chaste way that life is begotten is the way in which thoughts and ideas are born in the mind.

Finally, the thoughts of man are personal. Some thoughts of man are banal and commonplace, trite thoughts which no man remembers; but there are also thoughts which are spirit and life.

There are some thoughts of man into which man puts his very soul and his very being, all that he has been and all that he is, which thoughts are so much his own individual thoughts as to carry his personality and his spirit with them and to be recognizable as such.

Thus we say, "That is a thought of Pascal, of Bossuet, of Shakespeare, or of Dante."

Now apply these three reflections about human thought to God. God thinks a Thought, and that Thought is a Word; it is generated or born and is therefore called a Son, and finally, that Word or Son is Personal.

God thinks; He thinks a Thought. This Thought of God is a Word, as my own thought is called a word after it is pronounced. It is an internal word. But God's Thought is not like ours. It is not multiple.

God does not think one thought, or one word, one minute and another the next. Thoughts are not born to die, and do not die to be reborn in the mind of God. All is present to Him at once. In Him, there is only one word. He has no need of another.

That Thought or Word is infinite and equal to Himself, unique and absolute, firstborn of the Spirit of God; a Word from which all human words have been derived, and of which created things are merely the broken syllables or letters; a Word which is the source of all the wisdom in the world.

The latest scientific discoveries, the new knowledge of the great expanse of the heavens, the sciences of biology, physics, and chemistry, the more lofty sciences of metaphysics, philosophy, and theology—the knowledge of the shepherds, and the knowledge of the Wise Men—all this knowledge has its source in the Word or the Wisdom of God.

The infinite Thought of God is called not only a Word to indicate that it is the Wisdom of God, but it is also called a Son because it has been generated or begotten.

The Thought or the Word of God does not come from the outside world; it is born in His Spirit in a much more perfect way than the thought of "Justice" is generated by my spirit.

The giving of life or the power of birth, I repeat, is not limited to human beings. In the language of Sacred Scripture, "Shall not I, that make others to bring forth children, myself bring forth?" saith the Lord. "Shall I Who give generation to others myself be barren?" (Isa. 66:9).

The ultimate Source of all generation or birth is God, Whose Word is born of Him and therefore is called a Son.

Just as in our own human order, the principle of all generation is called the Father, so, too, in the Trinity the principle of all generation is called the Father, and the one generated is called the Son because He is the perfect Image and Resemblance of the Father.

If an earthly father can transmit to his son all the nobility of his character, and all the fine traits of his life, how much more so can the

Heavenly Father communicate to His own Eternal Son all the nobility, the perfection, and the eternity of His Being!

Finally, this Word or Son, begotten of the Eternal God, is personal. The thought of God is not commonplace, but reaches to the abyss of all that is known or can be known. Into this Thought of Word God puts Himself so entirely that it is as living as Himself.

If a human genius can put his whole personality into a thought, in a more perfect way God is able to put so much of Himself into a thought that that Thought or Word or Son is conscious of Himself and is a Divine Person.

The Father does not first exist and then think; the Father and Son are co-eternal, for in God all is present and unchanging.

Nothing is new and nothing is lost. Thus it is that the Father, contemplating His Image, His Word, His Son, can say in the ecstasy of the first and real paternity: "Thou art my son, this day have I begotten thee" (Ps. 2:9).

"This day"—this day of eternity, that is, the indivisible duration of being without end. "This day," in that act that will never end, as it has never begun; "this day"—the agelessness of eternity.

Go back to the origin of the world, pile century on century, aeon on aeon, age on age: "The Word was with God" (John 1:1). Go back before the creation of the angels, before Michael summoned his war hosts to victory with a flash of archangelic spears; even then, "The Word was with God."

It is that Word which St. John heard in the beginning of his Gospel, when he wrote: "In the beginning was the Word, and the Word was with God; and the Word was God" (John 1:1).

Just as my interior thoughts are not made manifest without a word, so the Word in the language of John, "was made flesh, and dwelt among us" (John 1:14).

And the Word is no other than the second Person of the Blessed Trinity, the Word who embraces the beginning and end of all things; the Word who existed before creation; the Word who presided at Creation as the King of the Universe, the Word made flesh at Bethlehem, the

Word made flesh on the Cross, and the Word made flesh dwelling in His divinity and humanity in the Eucharistic Emmanuel.

The Good Friday of twenty centuries ago did not mark the end of Him, as it did not mark the beginning. It is one of the moments of the Eternal Word of God.

Jesus Christ has a pre-history — a pre-history not to be studied in the rocks of the earth, nor in the caves of man, nor in the slime and dust of primeval jungles, but in the bosom of an Eternal Father.

He alone brought prehistory to history; He alone has dated all the records of human events into two periods: the period before, and the period after His coming.

If we would ever deny that the Word became flesh, and that the Son of God became the Son of Man, we would have to date our denial as over one thousand nine hundred years after His coming.

We are not yet finished with the inner life of God, for if God is the source of all life and truth and goodness in the world, He must have a will as well as an intellect; a love as well as a thought. It is a fact of nature that every being loves its own perfection.

The perfection of the eye is color, and it loves the beauty of the sun setting in the flaming monstrance of the west; the perfection of the ear is sound, and it loves the harmony of an overture of Beethoven or a sonata of Chopin.

Love has two terms: He who loves and He who is loved. In love the two are reciprocal. I love and I am loved. Between me and the one I love, there is a bond.

It is not my love; it is not his love; it is our love; the mysterious resultant of two affections, a bond which enchains, and an embrace wherein two hearts leap with but a single joy.

The Father loves the Son, the Image of His Perfection, and the Son loves the Father. Love is not only in the Father. Love is not only in the Son. There is something between them, as it were.

The Father loves the Son, whom He engenders. The Son loves the Father, who engendered Him. They contemplate each other; love each other in a love so powerful, so strong, and so perfect that it forms between them a living bond.

They give themselves in a love so infinite that, like the truth which expresses itself only in the giving of a whole personality, their love can express itself in nothing less than a Person, who is Love.

Love at such a stage does not speak; does not cry; does not express itself by words, nor by canticles; it expresses itself as we do in some ineffable moments, by that which indicates the very exhaustion of our giving: namely, a sigh, or a breath—and that is why the third Person of the Blessed Trinity is called the Holy Spirit or the Holy Ghost.

That breath of love is not a passing one as our own, but an Eternal Spirit. How all this is done, I know not, but on the testimony of God revealing, I know that this same Holy Spirit overshadowed the Blessed Virgin Mary, and He who was born of her was called the Son of God.

It was the same Spirit of whom our Lord spoke to Nicodemus when He told him he must be born again of "water and the Holy Ghost" (John 3:5).

It was the same Spirit Whom Our Blessed Savior gave to His apostles with the words, "Receive ye the Holy Ghost. Whose sins you shall forgive, they are forgiven them" (John 20:22–23).

It was the same Spirit of whom Our Lord spoke at the Last Supper: "He shall glorify me; because he shall receive of mine, and shall show it to you. All things whatsoever the Father hath, are mine" (John 16:14–15).

In this passage, Christ tells His disciples that the Holy Spirit, Who is to come, will in the future reveal Divine Knowledge which has been communicated to Him in His procession from both the Father and Son.

It is that same Spirit Who, in fulfillment of the promise, "when he, the Spirit of truth, is come, he will teach you all truth" (John 16:13), descended on the apostles on the day of Pentecost, and became the soul of the Church.

The continuous, unbroken succession of the truth communicated by Christ to His Church has survived to our own day, not because of the human organization of the Church, for that is carried on by frail vessels, but because of the profusion of the Spirit of Love and Truth over Christ's Vicar, and all who belong to Christ's Mystical Body, which is His Church.

Three in one, Father, Son, and Holy Ghost; three Persons in one God; one essence, distinction of Persons—such is the mystery of the Trinity; such is the inner life of God.

Just as I am, I know, and I love, and yet I am one; as the three angles of a triangle do not make three triangles but one; as the heat, power, and light of the sun do not make three suns, but one; as water, ice, and steam are all manifestations of the one substance; as the form, color, and perfume of the rose do not make three roses, but one; as our soul, our intellect, and our will do not make three substances, but one; as one times one times one times one does not equal three, but one—so, too, in some much more mysterious way, there are three Persons in God, and yet only one God.

The Trinity is the answer to the questions of Plato. If there is only one God, what does He think about? He thinks an eternal Thought, or about His Eternal Son. If there is only one God, whom does He love? He loves His Son, and that mutual love is the Holy Spirit.

The great philosopher was fumbling about for the mystery of the Trinity. His great mind seemed in some small way to suspect that an infinite being must have relations of thought and love, and that God cannot be conceived without thought and love.

But it was not until the Word became incarnate that man knew the secret of those relations and the inner life of God.

It is that mystery of the Trinity which gives the answer to those who have pictured God as an egotist God, sitting in solitary splendor before the world began, for the Trinity is a revelation that before creation God enjoyed the amiable society of His three Persons, the infinite communion with Truth and the embrace of infinite Love, and hence had no need ever to go outside Himself in search for happiness.

The greatest wonder of all is that, being perfect and enjoying perfect happiness, He ever should have made a world. If He did make a world, He could only have had one motive for making it. It could not add to His Perfection; it could not add to His Ttruth; it could not increase His Happiness. He made a world only *because He loved.*

Finally, it is the mystery of the Trinity which gives the answer to our quest for happiness and the true meaning of Heaven.

Heaven is not a place where there is the mere vocal repetition of alleluias or the monotonous fingering of harps. Heaven is a place where we find the fullness of the joys of earth.

Heaven is a place where we find in its plenitude those things which slake the thirst of hearts, satisfy the hunger of starving minds, and give rest to unrequited love.

Heaven is the communion with perfect Life, perfect Truth, and perfect Love, God the Father, God the Son, and God the Holy Ghost to whom be all honor and glory forever and ever. Amen.

God chose not to keep the secret of His Power to Himself, but told it to nothingness—and this was Creation. God chose not to keep the Beauty of His Intellect and Will, but to communicate a likeness of it to creatures—and these are angels and men.

Love wills not to keep the secrets of His Wisdom to Himself but tells them to man—and this is Revelation.

Love tends to become like the one loved, and since God loved man, God became man—and this is the Person of Jesus Christ, true God, and true man.

Love seeks to take another's pain and sin as its own and thus to make it whole—and this was the Cross and Redemption.

Love seeks not only to give what it has, but even to communicate its very Spirit—and this was Pentecost and the Birthday of the Church.

2

Some Characteristics of God's Love

The Love of God Is Justice!

How could God be good if He loved the bad equally with the good? The essence of love is not indifference to morality. "The way of the wicked is an abomination to the Lord: he that followeth justice is beloved by him" (Prov. 15:9).

"You have wearied the Lord with your words, and you said: Wherein have we wearied him? In that you say: Every one that doth evil, is good in the sight of the Lord, and such please him: or surely where is the God of judgment?" (Mal. 2:17)

The Love of God Is Freedom!

How could love be love if it were forced? By making man free, God made it possible for man to reject Divine Love. Man cannot be made to love God any more that he can be made to enjoy Bach's classical music. The power of choice is not necessarily the choice of what is best. Hence, "If you love me, keep my commandments" (John 14:15).

The Love of God Is the First Cause of All Things!

Though God is the First Cause of all things, man is a secondary and instrumental cause, and not a mere robot. God wrote a wonderful drama and gave it to free men to play, and sometimes they make a botch of it. Not in time, but at the end of the world, all things will be restored according to Justice. "For because sentence is not speedily pronounced against the evil, the children of men commit evils without any fear. But though a sinner do evil a hundred times, and by patience be borne withal, I know from thence that it shall be well with them that fear God, who dread his face" (Eccles. 8:11–12).

The Love of God Is Eternal!

Therefore, I can never escape it. I can tend toward it freely and thus receive mercy, or I can freely rebel against it and in my frustration feel His Justice. "For we must all be manifested before the judgment seat of Christ, that every one may receive the proper things of the body, according as he hath done, whether it be good or evil" (2 Cor. 5:10).

The Love of God Is All-Powerful!

God would never have given men the power to choose evil if He could not draw goodness out of evil. The power to crucify Christ is *mine*, but the effect of that crucifixion, namely, the conquest of death by resurrection, is not mine, but God's. "There is no wisdom, there is no prudence, there is no counsel against the Lord. The horse is prepared for the day of battle: but the Lord giveth safety" (Prov. 21:30–31).

The Love of God Is All-Seeing!

"Every man that passeth beyond his own bed, despising his own soul, and saying: Who seeth me? Darkness compasseth me about, and the walls cover me, and no man seeth me: whom do I fear? The Most High will not remember my sins. And he understandeth not that his eye seeth all things, for such a man's fear driveth from him the fear of God, and the eyes of man fearing him: And he knoweth not that the eyes of the Lord are far brighter.... For all things were known to the Lord God, before they were created: so also after they were perfected he beholdeth all things" (Sir. 23:25–29).

The Love of God Is Strong!

Love is not "broadmindedness." Capacity for indignation is sometimes a test of love, for there are enormities which true love must not only challenge, but resist. The sun which warms so gently can also wither; the rain which nourishes so tenderly can also rot. The change is not in the sun or the rain: it is in that upon which it falls. So the Love of God to the good is love; to the wicked, it seems wrath. "For we know that the judgment of God is, according to truth, against them that do such things.... Or despisest thou the riches of his goodness, and patience, and longsuffering? Knowest thou not that the benignity of God leadeth thee to penance? But according to thy hardness and impenitent heart, thou treasurest up to thyself wrath, against the day of wrath, and revelation of the just judgment of God" (Rom. 2:2, 4, 5).

The Love of God Is Merciful!

If we had never sinned, we never could have called Christ "Savior." "But thou hast mercy upon all, because thou canst do all things, and overlookest the sins of men for the sake of repentance. For thou lovest all things that are, and hatest none of the things which thou hast made: for thou didst not appoint, or make any thing hating it" (Wisd. 11:24–25).

The Love of God Is the Cause of Our Love!

There are sparks of love in us because there was first the Flame in God. "Jesus answered, and said to her: Whosoever drinketh of this water, shall thirst again; but he that shall drink of the water that I will give him, shall not thirst for ever: But the water that I will give him, shall become in him a fountain of water, springing up into life everlasting" (John 4:13–14).

The Love of God Rules the Universe

Because all things in the world, from atoms to angels, were made by Love, it follows that the whole universe seeks and moves toward its own perfection and its own good. Acorns tend to become good oaks; two atoms of hydrogen and one atom of oxygen united by an electrical spark tend to become water.

Inasmuch as all things have a natural inclination toward the perfection befitting their nature, they tend in some way to become like God. Scientists only *discover* the laws of nature; they do not *invent* them.

The chemical and biological laws which govern animals are all participations in the Eternal Reason and Love of God. They act for a purpose, that is, according to reason because Eternal Reason created them; they seek their own good because Eternal Goodness or Divine Love called them into being.

The Love of God Made a Moral Universe!

But Divine Love acted differently when He created man. Water *must* seek its own level, but man *ought* to be good. A stone cannot choose to fly upward when released from my hand, but a man can choose to disobey the law of his nature. In other words, lower nature is determined, and therefore amoral; man is free, and therefore moral.

God *compels* the stone to obey the law of gravitation, but He does not *compel* us to be good. How could we really love if we were forced?

Is it not the possibility of a No that gives so much charm to our Yes? God, therefore, gave us the power to seek deliberately a goal and purpose other than His Perfect Love, in order that there might be meaning in our allegiance and love when we freely choose to give it. To man alone on this earth did God communicate some of His Freedom.

And if it be asked: "If God knew that I would rebel against His love and be a sinner, why did He make me?" The answer is: God did not make you as a sinner. You made yourself a sinner. In that sense, you are your own creator.

The possibility, not the necessity, of moral evil, of wars and social injustices which follow them, is the price we have to pay for the greatest good we possess—the gift of freedom. God could, of course, at any moment stop a war, but only at a terrible cost—the destruction of human freedom.

There are only two things that could possibly remove evil and suffering from the world: either the conformity of human wills to the will of God, or God becoming a dictator and destroying all human wills.

Why is it that men, who by forgetting the Love of God turn the universe into a house of mass suicide, never think of blaming themselves, but immediately put God on the judgment seat, and question His Love and Goodness?

We all have a share in the evils of the world, and it ill behooves us to ignore our faults and become critics of God. It is we who are in the prisoners' dock in a world crisis like this. Instead of questioning the God of Love, we ought to be throwing ourselves on the Mercy of His Judgment.

3

Man Fleeing God's Love

These are several ways to avoid loving God:

Deny that you are a sinner.

Say that "no one believes in sin today" or "the sense of guilt is oppressive." If you are a fallen-away Catholic say: "I no longer believe in Confession."

Introduce speculative or theoretical questions to escape the implications of your moral bankruptcy and the primal, basic, inescapable fact that you have sinned against the love of God.

Thus you will avoid entertaining in your conscience the necessity of Confession.

This is what the woman at the well did when Our Lord, with a touch of moral realism, reminded her that she had five husbands. She evaded the issue of personal sin by raising the question of whether one ought to worship at Gerizim or Jerusalem.

Be like her. Make religion a controversy rather than a conversion. What you want is an argument, but what you need is absolution. By confusing the two, you can avoid meeting the God of love until the day of your death.

Pretend that religion is for the ignorant and the superstitious but not for the truly learned such as yourself.

Hearing Our Lord preaching in the Temple, some asked: "How doth this man know letters, having never learned?" (John 7:15). Here was the same snobbishness as in an earlier question: "Can any thing of good come from Nazareth?" (John 1:46).

Be concerned as they were, with the social background of those who teach religion, or with its intellectual tone rather than its *moral emphasis* and *spiritual intention*. Say that one religion is just as good as another, which is a clever way of implying that one is just as bad as another.

Boast of your "broadmindedness" and condemn the "intolerance" of everyone who has definite convictions. Dwell on no planet, but survey them all.

When religion must be discussed, always begin with, "Now this is *my* idea of religion," thus avoiding the problem of what is *God's* idea of religion. You thus reflect yourself in your own opinion.

Judge religions by whether they are "progressive" or "reactionary," "modern" or "medieval"; but never on the basis of whether they are "true" or "false." Boast of *where* you got your BA, rather than *what* you learned. Make it appear that your superior knowledge of comparative religions makes the comparison of religions useless.

Conceal the fact that in reality, you belong to the *intelligentsia*—those who have been educated beyond their intelligence.

Smile when you hear the text of Our Lord, "I praise Thee, Father, Lord of heaven and earth, because thou hast hidden these things from the wise and prudent, and hast revealed them to little ones" (Luke 10:21). And above all else when you wish to avoid discussing the spiritual life of the Catholic Church, libel it by saying it is "Fascist"!

Insist that the sole purpose of religion is social service.

When Our Lord fed the multitude, many crossed the lake to make Him King, but He answered: "Amen, amen I say to you, you seek me, not because you have seen miracles, but because you did eat of the loaves, and were filled. Labour not for meat which perisheth, but for that which endureth unto life everlasting, which the Son of Man will give you. For him hath God, the Father, sealed" (John 6:26–27).

But when He talked to them about Bread from Heaven, they said His religion was absurd. Life, they insisted, consists in being well fed. Think of religion solely as an "ambulance" to care for the economically unfed, until science and progress can dispense with it.

When the Church proposes a social solution based on spiritual regeneration, say, "The Church is political." When it abstains from a political policy, say, "The Church is too unworldly." Quote Marx: "Religion is the opium of the people."

Make it appear that Christianity is a means to social justice, rather than its cause. Above all else, condemn the Church for its attitude on artificial birth control. "After all, if God gave us bodies, He intended we should use them."

Then you escape that moral problem of the soul and render inapplicable the words of Our Lord: "For what doth it profit a man, if he gain the whole world, and suffer the loss of his own soul?" (Matt. 16:26). Of course, you will miss all the consolations of religion, for the Master said: "And fear ye not them that kill the body, and are not able to kill the soul: but rather fear him that can destroy both soul and body in hell" (Matt. 10:28).

Judge religion by whether or not it is accepted by the "important" people of the world.

When the masses crowded around Our Lord, the Pharisees sent ministers to apprehend Him. When the ministers returned empty-handed the Pharisees asked them: "Are you also seduced? Hath any one of the rulers believed in him, or of the Pharisees?" (John 7:47–48). They judged religion by the *elite* rather than by the *elect*.

Once, therefore, you become convinced of the truth of the Church, do not join it, lest you lose your job, or lest you be ridiculed by the world.

Some of the chiefs of the people believed in Our Lord, "but ... they did not confess Him.... For they loved the glory of men rather more than the glory of God" (John 12:42–43).

If an important man does embrace the Church, explain it away as "momentary insanity"; when a young woman enters the convent to dedicate her life to God, say: "She must have been disappointed in love." By so doing, you will always avoid discussing the eternal.

Concentrate on the idea that a Church which is not well received by the world cannot be true, thus avoiding the retort of the Savior: "I have chosen you out of the world, therefore the world hateth you" (John 15:19).

Avoid all contemplation, self-examination, and inquiry into the moral state of your soul.
Never be alone with yourself lest your conscience carry on an unbearable repartee. Cultivate a love of crowds, excitement, and noise. Thus will you be defended against "despairing scruples" and "silly qualms" and "remorse."

Shout down the whispers of Heaven. Alcohol may help extinguish the sparks of a few actual graces of God suggesting that you are not on the right track.

Make your business your religion, and then you will not have to make religion your business.

At night when you lie awake and are utterly alone with your soul, never give it a thought. Maybe you can escape the consequences of your life by not thinking about it.

If the thoughts of God get too strong, console yourself with the idea that "good" and "evil" are subjective and psychological. A good joke about Hell is always a good way to avoid dwelling on its possibility.

Call yourself a "heretic"; ridicule the pure as "Puritanical"; the clean of mouth as "devoid of a sense of humor"; but the best way of all to avoid serious thinking about religion is to say: "I've been through all that," as if there is nothing more to be said.

From that point on, the invitation of the Savior seems stupid: "Come to me, all you that labour, and are burdened, and I will refresh you. Take up my yoke upon you, and learn of me, because I am meek, and humble of heart: and you shall find rest to your souls. For my yoke is sweet and my burden light" (Matt. 11:28–30).

Take yourself very seriously.
Be proud of what you *have* rather than what you *are*; of what you *know* rather than what you *do*; of what you *did* rather than what you *ought to have done*.

If you cannot convince others that you know everything, then at least convince them that they know nothing. If you cannot lay claim to *omniscience*, you can probably make them admit their *nescience*.

There is no better way to keep God out of your soul than to be full of self. If you know all, how can God teach you anything? You escape the problem of faith by boasting of the capacities of your reason.

Say that you are too intelligent to believe in sin, and thus you avoid discussing redemption, for if you never did wrong, it is utterly stupid to suggest that someone could make you right.

Be a connoisseur of all churches in virtue of your superior wisdom, and you thus escape the obligation of joining any. Art critics do not paint. Why should religious critics be religious?

Keep your conceit always at a high level, for thus will you never be forced to admit that you are conceited. By the same token, you will succeed in identifying religion with infantilism.

You can even quote in your own support the words of Our Lord: "Amen I say to you, unless you turn and become as little children, you shall not enter into the kingdom of heaven. Whosoever, therefore, shall humble himself as this little child, he is the greater in the kingdom of heaven" (Matt. 18:3–4).

4

God's Love Pursuing Man

Though we may not always be on the quest of God, God is always on the quest of us. Even experiences and moments not of themselves calculated to spiritualize us, God in His Mercy may use to throw us back to Him. Thus:

Satiety

God calls the soul to Himself in the feeling of disgust. The very feeling following sin, the emptiness which sin engenders, God may use to summon us to be filled with His Grace.

An animal seeks pleasure within the finite limits of his physical organism; but man wants it to satisfy the infinite thirst of his soul. In man, therefore, the law of diminishing returns operates: As pleasure decreases, the desire for it increases. Pleasures then begin to exasperate because they "lie"; they do not give what they promised. Sadness, bitterness, and cynicism sometimes seize the soul, and with it a fatigue of life. That very emptiness can be the foundation of conversion. The desire for happiness could not be wrong. It must be, therefore, that we sought happiness in the wrong objects: in creatures apart from God, instead of in creatures under God's law. Thus, in the very confusion and disgust following sin is hidden a sense of awakened spiritual possibilities. A soul is on the verge of knowing itself when it knows that acting like a beast it *might* live like an angel. After having fed himself on husks, the prodigal began to yearn for the bread of the father's house.

Sacrifice

The self-indulgent soul which surrounds itself with every comfort and luxury, while making other persons means to its convenience, sometimes has its depths shattered by the sight of someone else living happily and peacefully amidst surroundings of complete self-forgetfulness and service for others. "I could be like that," or "I wish I were as happy as that person." The crust of egotism is broken and there gushes forth the awful beauty of self surrender. The soul for the first time comes to realize the sublime truth of Our Lord's words, that the best way to save life is to lose it. Such a consciousness is an actual grace of God, and if acted upon throws great light on the darkened cover of our soul.

Suffering

Many persons identify themselves with their environment. Because life is good to them, they believe they are good. They never dwell on eternity because time is so pleasant. When suffering strikes, they become divorced from their pleasant surroundings and are left naked in their own souls. They then see that they were not really affable and genial, but irritable and impatient. When the sun of outer prosperity sank, they had no inner light to guide their darkened souls. It is, therefore, not what happens to us that matters; it is how we react to it.

No one is better because of pain; conceivably a man may become seared and scarred by pain. But, the very emptiness of soul that follows enforced divorce from pleasurable surroundings does drive the soul back unto itself, and if it cooperates with grace at that moment, it may find the meaning of life. It was through a wound that St. Ignatius came to know himself. Many in life do not meet Christ until, like the thief on the right, they find Him on a Cross. On the battlefields in war many a man has found Him the only One to whom to turn.

Age

The young are full of hopes for life is full of promise. The sophomore thinks that science can take the place of God, that progress is necessary and not conditioned on discipline, and that pleasure is the goal of living. Later on, when one has left the hills of religion behind, and gone down into the plains where secular hopes were to be fulfilled, one becomes disillusioned by the monotony and routine of life. A moment comes when the soul begins to look back to those hills of religion, as to a happiness left behind. The fleeting years now seem to the soul as a thief in the house, explaining many losses which were never before. The soul is awakened; great possibilities lie ahead—for: "Not till the fire is dying in the grate, / Look we for any kinship with the stars."[1]

Impact with a Sinful World

All the modern explanations given for the existence of evil fail to fit the facts. Biologists told us evil was due to a fall in evolution, but if progress is inevitable why have there been two World Wars in twenty-one years?

Sociologists told us evil was due to systems: Capitalism or Communism or Nazism or Fascism. How could the world adopt evil systems if minds were not already fit soil for their growth? Since evil is so universal, must it not be due to a breakdown of a universal moral law? Is not the world in a mess for the same reason I am in a mess, namely, because I have not done what I *ought* to have done?

Is not this precisely what Christianity means, that God had to come down from Heaven to earth to make it right? Christianity does not begin in comfort but in catastrophe. Once a soul begins to realize that the world is rotten because it has broken the moral law of God, it has taken the first step toward conversion. God and the soul can meet on the roadway of a broken and disordered world. Such is the meaning of Bethlehem and Calvary.

[1] George Meredith, "Modern Love," 4, in *Poems*, vol. 1 (New York: Charles Scribner's Sons, 1910), 184.

Contact with the Divine Presence

Sometimes it has happened that a man who had never given a thought to religion entered a Catholic church and although he knew nothing of her teaching, after half an hour or more spent in the presence of the Blessed Sacrament, was seized with a sense that "Something or Someone is there" that makes the church different. Such a soul does not know or believe that Our Lord is really and truly present on the altar of every Catholic church. He does know that he feels "impelled" to remain in that mysterious Presence. Like the disciples of Emmaus, the soul has been companioning with the Savior without knowing it. The investigation of the reasons behind the sense of the sacred in this and similar experiences may lead to the fullness of faith.

Sadness

Why do we love to see, on the stage or screen, doleful and tragical things which we never would want to befall us? Why should sorrow be our pleasure and tears be our satisfaction? Why do we weep for the fanciful on the stage, but not for the reality? Why do we, who would have none of our friends murdered, love to read about murders? Do men who are at peace want to see feigned misery? Do those who are glad rejoice in pretended tragedy?

Is not our desire to see that which is sad or tragic a revelation of the sadness and tragedy of our own souls? A soul that loves God and sees misery wants to relieve it; a soul that has abandoned God and sees misery wants to weep over it, not knowing that he is really weeping over himself. We act as mourners when we really are the mourned.

The moment we realize that our sadness is born of our sins, we are ripe for conversion. Then we feel the poignancy of the invitation: "Come to me, all you that labour, and are burdened, and I will refresh you" (Matt. 11:28).

O Whither Shall I Fly

O Whither shall I fly? what path untrod
Shall I seek out to 'scape the flaming rod
Of my offended, of my angry God?...

'Tis vain to *flee*; 'tis neither here nor there
Can 'scape that hand, until that hand forbear;
Ah me! where is he not, that's ev'rywhere?

'Tis vain to flee, till gentle mercy show
Her better eye; the farther off we go,
The swing of Justice deals the mightier blow.

The ingenuous child, corrected, doth not fly
His angry mother's hand, but clings more high,
And quenches with his tears her flaming eye....

Great God! there is no safety here below;
Thou art my fortress, thou that seem'st my foe.
'Tis thou, that strik'st the stroke, must guard the blow.

Thou art my God, by thee I fall or stand;
Thy grace hath given me courage to withstand
All tortures, but my conscience and thy hand.

I know thy justice is thyself; I know,
Just God, thy very self is mercy too;
If not to thee, where, whither shall I go?

—Francis Quarles[2]

[2] Francis Quarles, "Job 14:13," "Emblems" 12 in *The Complete Works in Prose and Verse of Francis Quarles*, vol. 3, ed. Alexander B. Grosart (St. George's: Edinburgh University Press, 1881), 75–76.

The Pulley

When God at first made man,
Having a glass of blessings standing by,
"Let us," said He, "pour on him all we can;
Let the world's riches, which dispersed lie,
Contract into a span."

So strength first made a way;
Then beauty flow'd, then wisdom, honour, pleasure;
When almost all was out, God made a stay,
Perceiving that, alone of all His treasure,
Rest in the bottom lay.

"For if I should," said He,
"Bestow this jewel also on My creature,
He would adore My gifts instead of me,
And rest in Nature, not the God of Nature:
So both should losers be.

"Yet let him keep the rest,
But keep them with repining restlessness;
Let him be rich and weary, that at least,
If goodness lead him not, yet weariness
May toss him to My breast."

—George Herbert

If I Could Shut the Gate

If I could shut the gate against my thoughts
And keep out sorrow from this room, within,
Or memory could cancel all the notes
Of my misdeeds, and I unthink my sin:
How free, how clear, how clean my soul should lie,
Discharged of such a loathsome company!
Or were there other rooms without my heart

That did not to my conscience join so near,
Where I might lodge the thoughts of sin apart
That I might not their clamorous crying hear,
What peace, what joy, what ease should I possess,
Freed from their horrors that my soul oppress!
But, O my Saviour, Who my refuge art,
Let Thy dear mercies stand 'twixt them and me,
And be the wall to separate my heart
So that I may at length repose me free;
That peace, and joy, and rest may be within,
And I remain divided from my sin.

—Anonymous

5

Divine Friendship

Though man is human, he may live on a threefold level: subhuman, human, and divine.

The Subhuman Level

We never say to a monkey when he acts foolish: "Do not act like a nut," because the monkey has not the power to lower himself to a sub-monkey level. But to a man, we can say: "Do not act like a monkey," because a man sometimes can fail to be all that he *ought* to be; he can lower himself to a subhuman level. A fall from a higher state is not possible to the beast, but it is possible for man; a monkey can never be a nut, but a man can be a beast.

Man lives on this subhuman level in several ways: When he denies he has a soul and thus identifies himself with the animal; when he affirms that he has no other destiny than to disintegrate with the dust; and when he bases his life on the principle that the sole purpose of living is the satisfaction of his animal impulses.

The Human Level

A man begins to live a human existence when he recognizes a *specific* difference between himself and animals, namely, possession of an intellect which can understand Truth and a will which can choose Goodness. As a human being, he bends subhuman things to his will; for example, he makes his body the servant of his soul, and he makes his soul subject to God. He knows that he is smaller than the cosmos, but he refuses to be intimidated by it, knowing that he is bigger than the cosmos because he can get the Heavens into his head by understanding its laws. That leaves him one supreme task: To get his head into the Heavens. On this human level, man knows that he came from God and that to God he must return. Hence the universe is to be viewed sacramentally as a material thing to be used for the purpose of leading the good life.

The Divine Level

Living on the human level is not very satisfactory, not only because reason is limited, and the will weak, but also because, on this human level, our relations to God are not clear.

As it is possible for man to sink below the human level, so it is also possible for him to be raised above it. This he cannot do by his own power. A crystal cannot become a flower, nor can man become a child of God by his own unaided effort. No moral effort, no evolutionary process, no intensification of philanthropy can lift man to the spiritual level by which he participates in the Life of God.

The plant cannot live in the animal unless the animal takes it up into its kingdom. In a more rigid way, man cannot live in God and share His Divine Life unless the Divine Life comes down and lifts him up to its level. One cannot live a human life unless born to it, and one cannot live a divine life unless born to it. Between the human and the divine level there is a law on guard: The law that life comes from life, and God-life comes from God. "Amen, amen I say to thee, unless a man be born again of water and the Holy Ghost, he cannot enter into the kingdom of God" (John 3:5). This birth on the divine level is the Sacrament of Baptism.

By being "born again" of the spirit and not of the flesh, we are lifted to the *super*-natural level, one to which we are no more entitled by nature than a rose is entitled to hearing, or a dog is entitled to speech.

Naturally, we are creatures of God; supernaturally, we are children of God. In the natural order, God is Creator, Providence, or the End of man. In the supernatural order, God the Father is our Creator, God the Son our Redeemer, and God the Holy Spirit our Sanctifier.

This mystical unity with God, which is born in our soul in Baptism, is actualized by Faith, Hope, and Charity, and is increased by gifts of the Holy Spirit and the Sacraments. Thus it is evident that though union with God is a free gift, it cannot be preserved nor increased *without our cooperation*. I might wake up some morning and discover I had suddenly been infused with the gift of playing the piano; but unless I practiced from that point on, I could lose the gift. Similarly, the gift of faith must not be left barren.

There are ultimately only two possible theories to account for the nature and the origin of man: One is that the life of man is a push from below; the other, that the life of man is a gift from above. The one is that man is wholly of the earth, earthly; the other that he is partly of the Heaven, Heavenly. The second is the Christian conception: man is not a risen beast, he is rather a kind of fallen angel. His origin is hidden not in the slime and dust of prehistoric forests, but in the clear daylight of Paradise where he communed with God; his origin goes back not to cosmic forces, but to Divine Grace. According to this conception, man is supposed to act not like a beast because he came from one, but like God, because he is made to His own image and likeness.

Which of these two views of man is nobler? The one which regards him as a little biochemical entity of flesh and blood, only about six feet tall, apt to be killed by a microbe, standing self-poised and self-centered in such a universe as this, acknowledging in self-conceit no God, no purpose, no future, and still hoping that the blind cosmic forces of space and time will sweep him on until he becomes lost in the bursting of the great cosmic bubble? Or the other view which shows us that same being awakened to his own actual sinfulness, his possible saintliness; his own actual humanity, his possible sharing in the life of Christ; his enrolling himself, by an act of self-distrust, which is the highest kind of self-assertion, under no less a person than the Son of God, made man, and crying out directly to the Lord of the universe, "I am thine, O God. O help me whom Thou hast made."

When a man answers this question correctly, he will understand something of the true nature of man and the love of God who came to restore the gifts which man had lost, and in gratitude, his heart will cry out: "My God! My God! What is a heart, that Thou shouldst it so eye, and woo, pouring upon it all Thy art, as if Thou hadst nothing else to do?"[3]

After Christ's Ascension into Heaven, how did this Fountainhead of Divine Life communicate that Life to man? He communicated it in the same way He communicated His Truth, and His Power, namely, through His Mystical Body, the Church. Since He had chosen a human nature as the instrument for the sanctification of men during His historical life, so would He use a corporation of human natures as the instrument for the sanctification of men until the end of time.

Just as the invisible energy of my brain descends into all parts of my body, giving movements to arms and legs, muscles and sinews, so there descend beams of grace from the glorified Christ to the members of His Mystical Body. He even went so far as to determine the precise manner in which He would sanctify souls in His Mystical Body, the Church; namely, through the Sacraments.

What Is a Sacrament?

In the broad sense, a sacrament is a material, visible thing used as a channel for the spiritual and the invisible. The world is made up of sacraments of the natural order. A handshake is a sacrament, in the sense that it is a visible clasping of hands to express the invisible; namely, welcome and friendship.

Baptism

How many sacraments has Christ chosen to vivify His Mystical Body? Since the supernatural life is modeled upon human life, we might expect

3 George Herbert, "Matins."

the number to be seven, and such it actually is. But why seven? Because there are seven conditions upon which life is possible; five which condition our individual life, and two which condition our social life.

In the individual order, the first condition of all life is birth, for obviously unless I am born, I cannot live. In the supernatural order, too, unless I am born to Christ, I cannot live His Life—and this is the Sacrament of Baptism.

Confirmation

Secondly, in the natural order, a man must not only be born but he must also grow from infancy to maturity. In the supernatural order, a soul must grow to spiritual maturity as a perfect cell in the Mystical Body, so that it may overcome obstacles which stand in the way of that Divine Life—and this is the Sacrament of Confirmation.

The Eucharist

Thirdly, in order to live naturally, a life must nourish itself. In the supernatural order, a soul must nourish the Divine Life already within it—and this is the Sacrament of the Eucharist.

Penance

Fourthly, in the natural order, it sometimes happens that a part of the body may become injured, in which case the wound must be bound and healed. In the supernatural order, it sometimes happens that a soul may sin, in which instance a member of the Mystical Body becomes wounded, or even dies. The spiritual wound must be healed and the inanimate member revivified—and this is the Sacrament of Penance.

Extreme Unction

Fifthly, the last condition of individual life in the natural order is the overcoming of the effects of disease, for a body may not only be wounded, it may suffer from the physical weakness which follows a disease. In the supernatural order, the soul must be freed from the remains of sin, or the moral weakness which comes in the wake of sin—and this is the Sacrament of Extreme Unction.

Matrimony

Now to pass to the two other conditions of life which affect us as social beings—for we are not only individuals but also members of society. In the natural order, society is conditioned upon the procreation of our species. In the supernatural order, too, the growth of the Mystical Body is conditioned upon the raising up of children of God—and this is through the Sacrament of Matrimony.

Holy Orders

Finally, as a social being, man must also be governed. This implies officials whose business it is to apply the fruits of law and order to their neighbors. In the supernatural order, too, the members of the Mystical Body must also be governed. This implies ministers in order that the effects of the Redemption may be applied to souls—this is through the Sacrament of Holy Orders.

Living with God

The seven Sacraments are thus channels through which Christ in Heaven builds up His Mystical Body on earth by the infusion of His Divine Life. They are the bridges between Christians and Christ in His Glory; the channels through which the waters of everlasting life pour forth into the garden of the soul. The Sacraments are the kisses of God under the visible sign of which He floods the soul with the riches of His Love.

"What effect can a little water have which is poured on the head of a child?" Judge not the existence of those divine outpourings by the matter you see in the Sacraments, which are but the sign of the life within; judge not Baptism by the water, or the Eucharist by the bread, any more than you judge the joy of friendship by a handshake or an embrace.

What is the spoken word but soundwaves put in movement? But when the soul is in it, it becomes eloquence, justice, truth, courage to do and die! Think, then, of what a word is when God puts *His Soul* into it!

What is water but a union of hydrogen and oxygen? Put the genius of man into it and it becomes vapor, commerce, power, civilization. Think then what water is when God puts Himself into it!

What is bread but the mere chemical combination of wheat, water, and yeast? Unite it with the soul of man, and it becomes food, strength, life, joy. Think then of what bread is when God unites His Life with it!

And with the other sacraments; that which strikes the eye in them is weak and poor, but that which strikes the soul is divine.

The Sacraments are the normal channels by which the Divine Life is poured into our souls. Once we are made "partakers of the divine nature" (2 Pet. 1:4), God becomes present to us in a new way. He is present not only in the universe by His Power, His Wisdom, and His Goodness. He is present not only in the tabernacle where He dwells in His Body and Blood, Soul and Divinity, under the form of bread; but He is also present in the soul. What causes God to be there? Grace. What can expel Him from there? Sin.

What does this Presence of God in our souls by grace make us? Three things:

A Temple of God

> If any one love me, he will keep my word, and my Father will love him, and we will come to him, and will make our abode with him. (John 14:23)
>
> Know you not, that you are the temple of God, and that the Spirit of God dwelleth in you? (1 Cor. 3:16)

Another Christ by Participation

And I live, now not I; but Christ liveth in me. And that I live now in the flesh: I live in the faith of the Son of God, who loved me, and delivered himself for me. (Gal. 2:20)

Adopted Sons of God

Jesus Christ is the natural Son of God made man. We are only the adopted sons. But because we are sons we have a right to be fed: "Father, give us this day our daily bread" (see Matt. 6:11). Because we are sons, we have a right to the Father's indulgence: "Father, forgive us our trespasses" (see Matt. 6:12). Because we are sons, we are heirs of the Kingdom of Heaven. If therefore we are in the state of grace, or possess that similitude to the Divine Nature, Our Lord will say to us at death: "Come, ye blessed of my Father, possess you the kingdom prepared for you from the foundation of the world" (Matt. 25:34).

How did we acquire the right to be lifted from the human level of creatures to the superhuman level of children of God? Through the love of the Father who from all eternity chose us and predestined us to be conformable to the image of His Son. Through the love of the Son who, becoming man and dying for us on Calvary, broke down the wall of sin which divided us from God and redeemed us by His death on the Cross: "In whom we have redemption through his blood, the remission of sins, according to the riches of his grace" (Eph. 1:7). Through the love of the Holy Spirit, who incorporated us to Christ in Baptism: "And such some of you were; but you are washed, but you are sanctified, but you are justified in the name of our Lord Jesus Christ, and the Spirit of our God" (1 Cor. 6:11).

Why Is Sin Wrong?

Because sin is a divorce of man from the Divine Life in the soul. What death is to the body, that sin is to the soul. "For the wages of sin is death"

(Rom. 6:23). Man in the state of grace has a double "life." The life of the body is the soul; the life of the soul is grace. When the soul leaves the body, the body dies. When grace leaves the soul, the soul dies. This is a "double death." That is why the greatest tragedy in the world is to die in the state of sin.

Renunciation

Why must the Christian renounce himself by mortification and penance? Original Sin was destroyed in our soul by Baptism, but the possibility of actual sin continues. Death is a masterpiece, and no masterpiece was ever made in a day. If therefore we are to die well, that is, in the love of God—we must learn to "die" often during life by renouncing all those things which might injure the love of God in our souls.

Since I am one with Christ by grace, what ought to be my disposition of soul? A constant desire to put on the mind of Christ so that I think about things from "His point of view," so that I will the things which He wills. Before doing any deed I should ask: 'Will this be pleasing to God?" As St. Elizabeth of the Trinity said: "We must become an additional humanity for Christ,"[4] that is, so putting ourselves at the disposal of Our Lord that He may work through us, as His Sacred Humanity was always at the disposal of the Word.

Glory to God

At what moment do Catholics render most glory to God? In the Holy Sacrifice of the Mass. For no man can glorify God as He deserves, except Our Lord because He is the Son of God and the Son of Man. Therefore, He is the Mediator between God and man. The only true worship of God is through Christ, and it is in the Mass that Jesus Christ is offered to the

[4] See "Prayer to the Holy Trinity," Carmelite Monastery of Rochester, Discalced Carmelites of Rochester, https://carmelitesofrochester.org/new-page-82.

Father—but not Jesus Christ alone. We are with Him. The work of the Savior is sufficient only for him who completes it on his own account. In the Mass, we unite ourselves to the offering Christ made of Himself upon the Cross. When He died on the Cross, we died with Him. "For the charity of Christ presseth us: judging this, that if one died for all, then all were dead" (2 Cor. 5:14).

For this mystical renewal of Christ's death in the Mass to take place effectually in each of us, we must unite ourselves to it. And how are we to become victims with this Supreme Victim? By yielding ourselves, like Him, to the entire accomplishment of the Divine Will. We must be in the essential attitude of giving *all* to God, of so uniting our mortifications, penances, and trials to His that we may be able to say, as Our Lord did on the eve of His Passion: "But that the world may know, that I love the Father: and as the Father hath given me commandment, so do I: Arise, let us go hence" (John 14:31)—that is, to Calvary.

6

Ways of Preserving Friendships

We can never be a true friend of anyone whom we do not know. Few of us really know ourselves, and few ever want to know. We imagine ourselves to be very different from what we are. We wear a mask in public but seldom take it off when we are alone. Hence we think that our critics *always* misjudge us. We believe our friends are right when they praise us and wrong when they criticize us. Most of our acquaintances could tell us faults about ourselves which we would deny most vociferously, and yet they might be only too true.

Know Thyself

For a good reason, therefore, the Greeks inscribed on the Temple of Apollo at Delphi the injunction: "Know thyself." Plutarch added: "If the 'Know thyself' of the oracle were an easy thing for every man, it would not be held to be a divine injunction."[5]

The Divine Savior in telling the story of the Prodigal Son marked the moment of the latter's conversion with the words: "Returning to himself, he said," etc. (Luke 15:17).

[5] *Plutarch's Lives*, vol. 7, *Demosthenes and Cicero; Alexander and Caesar*, ed. E. Capps, T.E. Page, and W.H.D. Rouse (New York: G.P. Putnam's Sons, 1919), 7.

Self-knowledge is not intellectual, but moral. It falls not within the domain of psychology, but theology; it is concerned not with what we think, but with our motives and the hidden springs of life and action.

Self-examination must be done in the presence of God—we must compare ourselves *not* with our *neighbor*, nor with our own subjective ideals, but with the Perfect. How often in life we stand self-revealed by coming in contact with a noble life. In self-examination, it is God and not man who makes us enter into ourselves. As Simeon said when he held the Babe: "This child is set ... that out of many hearts, thoughts may be revealed" (Luke 2:34, 35).

In that wondrous Presence, there can be room neither for hidden pride nor barren hopelessness.

Bewilderment

The neurotic, the bewildered, and the disillusioned are today flocking to psychoanalysts to have their minds analyzed, when what they really need is to go to God to have their sins forgiven.

There can be no health of soul or body while there is a moral conflict within. The modern mind thought it got rid of Hell but found it within. A psychoanalyst can sublimate; God alone can give peace.

As Dr. Jung, the celebrated psychoanalyst, admitted: "About a third of my cases are suffering from no clinically definable neurosis, but from the senselessness and emptiness of their lives.... This can well be described as the general neurosis of our time."[6] "A considerable number [of patients] came to see me not because they were suffering from a neurosis but because they could find no meaning in their lives."[7]

[6] Carl Gustav Jung, *Modern Man in Search of a Soul*, trans. W. S. Dell and Cary F. Baynes (New York: Kegan Paul, Trench, Trübner and Company, 2005), 62.

[7] Carl Gustav Jung, *Psychology and Western Religion*, trans. R. F. C. Hull (New York: Routledge, 2014), 204.

Lives are disordered and unhappy because they are *multiple*. Like broken mirrors, they reflect a hundred different objects, but no single purpose which could give unity to life. Our Lord asked the name of the devil who possessed the soul of the young man, and the devil answered: "Legion." He had lost his unity.

One of the reasons of this tension *within* is because we have never settled absolutely for ourselves whether our body or our soul should dominate. If we concentrate on the pleasures of the body, we surrender the joys of the soul. If we concentrate on the soul, we make the body its servant, and therefore a sharer in the joys of the soul. So long as we are without a goal of living, we are like a radio tuned in to two different stations, getting no harmony but only static, no enjoyment but only a feeling of irritation.

Goal of Living

What is the goal of human living? That question has already been answered: To attain Perfect Life without death, Truth without error, and Love without hate or satiety—which is God.

A man is happy when he fulfills the end for which he is made. Creatures of all kinds—gold, food, machinery, flesh, money—are means to attain God. It is making them the *ends* of life which constitutes selfishness and causes sin and disorder. This comes so easily to our fallen natures that we must constantly be on our guard. To this end, a self-examination should be made every night before retiring and should be followed by a prayer expressing sorrow for our sins, asking God for forgiveness, and resolving to amend our ways and to do penance for the sins we have committed.

This examination can be very brief. It should revolve around the seven capital sins, the seven pallbearers of the soul:

Pride

Pride is an inordinate love of one's own excellence and, as such, it dethrones God from the soul and enthrones "I." "No God, no Master. I am God. I am my own Lord." Every proud person takes himself too seriously.

Human beings are like sponges. Each human being can stand so much honor, as a sponge can hold so much water. Both quickly reach a point of saturation. When a sponge passes that point, it drips; when a man passes that point, the honor wears him instead of him wearing the honor.

The proud person exaggerates his own personal qualities, talks about himself, his accomplishments, is jealous of everyone else—as if others, by gaining an honor, had stolen it from him. Associated with this is constant fault-finding.

The envious never know that their criticism of others is vicarious self-criticism. The man who accuses another of infidelity, jealousy, or pride is generally guilty of those sins himself. Thus he projects to others his own faults and is judged in his judgment of others.

Have I attributed to my own judgment a higher value than the Wisdom of God, or His Moral Law, or the Christian tradition, or the teaching of His Church?

Have I presumed to pass judgment on religious doctrines which I hardly understood?

Have I drawn others into sin by sneering that God's law was out of date, or was impossible, or old-fashioned?

How can God fill me with His Grace if I am already filled with self?

Do I realize that any talents or gifts I have received came from God, and therefore I ought to thank Him? "For who distinguisheth thee? Or what hast thou that thou hast not received? And if thou hast received, why dost thou glory, as if thou hadst not received it?" (1 Cor. 4: 7).

Do I always seek to be seen? Do I seek notoriety or publicity as if the be-all and end-all of life were to be known by men? "But when thou are invited, go, sit down in the lowest place; that when he who invited thee, cometh, he may say *to* thee: Friend, go up higher. Then shalt thou have glory before them that sit at table with thee" (Luke 14:10).

Do I ever practice humility or recognize the truth about myself? "Take up my yoke upon you, and learn of me, because I am meek, and humble of heart: and you shall find rest to your souls" (Matt. 11:29).

Avarice

Avarice is the inordinate love of earthly goods. Undue love of money gives a man a "heart of gold"—cold and yellow.

Do I seek wealth regardless of the rights of others?

Do I spend superfluities only on myself or for my own pleasure; for example, for drink, entertainment, etc., instead of on others, that is, the poor, the sick, or on churches for the poor?

Do I advertise to enlarge my business rather than pay a living wage to my employees?

Have I over a long period of time refused to give alms to the poor, the needy, or the afflicted?

Do I realize that on the day of my death the only possessions I really will have will be those I gave away, for their merit will still be with me?

Have I pondered on the words of Our Lord: "Lay not up to yourselves treasures on earth: where the rust, and moth consume, and where thieves break through and steal. But lay up to yourselves treasures in heaven: where neither the rust nor moth doth consume, and where thieves do not break through, nor steal" (Matt. 6:19–20)?

Seek ye therefore first the kingdom of God, and his justice, and all these things shall be added unto you. (Matt. 6:33)

Envy

Envy is discontent with another's good, a mentality which is cast down at another's good, as if it were an affront to our own superiority.

Do I assert my envy by "running down" others by innuendo, half-truths, fault-finding, or by attributing to them false motives?

Have I rejoiced over the misfortunes of others?

Have I ever tried to cure my jealousy by praying for the one of whom I was jealous?

Why have I not made the quality of a neighbor an occasion for imitation rather than envy, and thus increased in some way the welfare of humanity and the glory of God: "But if you bite and devour one another; take heed you be not consumed one of another" (Gal. 5:15).

Is my sympathy for the needy inspired by love of the poor or by hatred of the rich?

Anger

Unjust anger is a violent and inordinate desire to punish others and is often accompanied by hatred which seeks not only to repel aggression, but to take revenge.

Am I impatient with others? Do I buy into "fits of temper" and make cutting and sarcastic remarks because my will has been crossed?

Do I find excuses for being provoked at my neighbor but never admit the same excuse for him being provoked at me?

Do I ever practice patience, that is, think before I speak, then talk to myself?

Have I ever asked myself how will God forgive my sins if I do not forgive the faults of others?

Do I realize that being quickly aroused to anger is a sign of selfishness, and that my character is known from the things I hate? If I love God, I will hate sin; if I love sin, I will hate religion. "Judge not, that you may not be judged" (Matt. 7:1).

Gluttony

Gluttony is the abuse of the lawful pleasure God has attached to eating and drinking, which are necessary conditions of self-preservation. It becomes sinful when it incapacitates us for the fulfillment of our duties, injures our health, endangers the interests of others, or when—for Catholics—it breaks the laws of fast and abstinence.

Have I made others suffer as a result of intoxication? Have I, a Catholic, broken the laws of the Church concerning fast and abstinence?

Have I encouraged others to drink more than was good for them?

Do I advert to the fact that the principal danger of the "cocktail hour" and frequentation of bars is not complete intoxication, but the materialization of life and the loss of spiritual values?

Do I appreciate that God's gifts of food and drink and other necessities are *means*, not ends; that is, that they are given for the renewal of my strength, that I might place myself in His service? "Therefore, whether you eat or drink, or whatsoever else you do, do all to the glory of God" (1 Cor. 10:31).

Sloth

Sloth is a malady of the will which causes us to neglect our duties. It is physical sloth when it manifests itself in laziness, procrastination, idleness, and indifference. It is spiritual sloth when it shows a distaste for the things of the spirit, a hurrying of devotions, a religious lukewarmness, and a failure to cultivate new virtues.

Do I accept ready-made opinions from propagandists, instead of thinking them out for myself in the perspective of history and ethics?

Do I excuse myself from taking Christianity seriously on some such ill-considered ground as that the Christ-life is unacceptable to twentieth-century standards?

Do I do any serious reading to improve my spiritual condition?

Have I been neglectful of my duties to God?

Do I pray?

> And withal being idle they learn to go about from house to house: and are not only idle, but tattlers also, and busybodies, speaking things which they ought not. (1 Tim. 5:13)

Lust

Lust is an inordinate love of the pleasures of the flesh. God attached pleasure to eating and drinking that the individual life might be preserved; He also attached great pleasure to the marital act in order that social life and the Kingdom of God might be preserved.

The pleasure becomes sinful when used as an exclusive end rather than a means. Lust, for that reason, is perverted love. It looks not to the good of the other, but to the pleasure of self. It breaks the glass that holds the wine, and smashes the lute to snare the music.

Have I consented to evil thoughts?

If it is wrong to do a certain thing, must I not also refuse to think about that thing? "Whosoever shall look on a woman to lust after her, hath already committed adultery with her in his heart" (Matt. 5:28).

Have I encouraged others to sin by thought, word, or deed?

Have I violated purity by thought, word, or deed? Have I tried to cultivate a higher love, and thus sublimate a lower?

Honesty is a burden only to those who have lost the sense of others' rights, and purity is a burden for the same reason.

> Know you not, that you are the temple of God, and that the Spirit of God dwelleth in you? (1 Cor. 3:16)

> All things are clean to the clean: but to them that are defiled, and to unbelievers, nothing is clean: but both their mind and their conscience are defiled. (Titus 1:15)

> Dearly beloved, I beseech you as strangers and pilgrims, to refrain yourselves from carnal desires which war against the soul. (1 Pet. 2:11)

> I beseech you therefore, brethren, by the mercy of God, that you present your bodies a living sacrifice, holy, pleasing unto God, your reasonable service. (Rom. 12:1)

> Blessed are the clean of heart: for they shall see God. (Matt. 5:8)

7

Disciplining Myself for Love

I Am a Child of God

We become children of God and heirs of Heaven by being "reborn" in the Sacrament of Baptism. But to proceed from this ordinary unconscious union of grace to an evergrowing union of will requires, among other things, a certain amount of self-discipline. In order that the spirit may not be in bondage to the flesh, the flesh must be subdued, without ever annihilating it or destroying our nature.

Self-discipline may be defined as a struggle against evil inclinations in order to subject them to our own will and ultimately to the will of God.

The modern world is opposed to self-discipline on the ground that personality must be "self-expressive." Self-expression is right so long as it does not end in self-destruction. A boiler that would be self-expressive by blowing up, or an engine that would be self-expressive by jumping the tracks, would both be acting contrary to their natures as fashioned by the minds of the engineers who designed them. So, too, if man acts contrary to what is best and highest in his nature by rebelling against the Eternal Reason of God, his Creator, his self-expression is self-destruction.

We have a body and we have a soul. Each has different satisfactions; the pleasures of one militate against the pleasures of the other. Each has a different landing field. Tension, neurosis, and unhappiness come from the attempt to satisfy both. "No man can serve two masters" (Matt. 6:24). "For he that will save his life, shall lose it: and he that shall lose his life for my sake, shall find it" (Matt. 16:25).

The condition of being a true Christian is to be self-disciplined. "If any man will come after me, let him deny himself, and take up his cross daily, and follow me" (Luke 9:23). "For if you live according to the flesh, you shall die: but if by the Spirit you mortify the deeds of the flesh, you shall live" (Rom. 8:13). "And they that are Christ's, have crucified their flesh, with the vices and concupiscences" (Gal. 5:24). So, "if thy right eye scandalize thee, pluck it out and cast it from thee. For it is expedient for thee that one of thy members should perish, rather than thy whole body be cast into hell" (Matt. 5:29).

Love

Love is the inspiration of all sacrifice. Love is not the desire to have, to own, to possess—that is selfishness. Love is the desire to be had, to be owned, to be possessed. It is the giving of oneself for another.

The symbol of love, as the world understands it, is the circle continually surrounded by self, thinking only of self. The symbol of love, as Christ understands it, is the Cross with its arms outstretched even unto eternity to embrace all souls within its grasp.

Sinful love, as the world understands it, finds its type in Judas the night of the betrayal: "What will you give me, and I will deliver him unto you" (Matt. 26:15). Love in its true sense finds its type in Christ a few hours later when, mindful of His disciples, He says to the friends of the traitor who blistered His lips with a kiss, "If therefore you seek me, let these go their way" (John 18:8).

Love is the giving of self. So long as we have a body and are working out our salvation, love will always be synonymous with sacrifice, in the Christian sense of the word.

Love sacrifices naturally, just as the eye sees naturally and the ear hears naturally. That is why we speak of "arrows" and "darts" of love—something that wounds.

The bridegroom who loves will not give to his bride a ring of tin or of brass, but the best he can obtain—platinum, if he can afford it, because the gold or platinum ring represents sacrifice; it costs something.

The mother who sits up all night nursing her sick child does not call it hardship, but love.

The day men forget that love is synonymous with sacrifice, they will ask, "What a selfish sort of woman it must be who ruthlessly extracts tribute in the form of flowers," just as they do ask, "What cruel kind of God is it who asks for sacrifice and self-denial?" Love is the reason of all immolation.

Hence, the man who loves his perfected life in Christ will die to himself—and this dying to himself, this taming of his members as so many wild beasts, this being imprinted with the Cross, is mortification.

Discipline

Keep the imagination under control. You can imagine a mountain of gold, but you will never own one. The imagination promises what it can never deliver on this earth.

Know how to refuse. By consenting to every common impulse and the pleasure of every sense, one becomes a "Yes man" to the voice of self-destruction. Our character is made by our choices.

The purpose of discipline is charity. Mortification is a means to the love of God and neighbor, and not an end in itself. The gifts of God are our servants. It is when they become rebel servants, or our masters, that we need to tame them.

In self-discipline, you "give up" nothing. You merely "exchange." You find that you can get along without an excess of drink, but you cannot give up peace of mind or union with God so you "exchange" one for another. "What exchange shall a man give for his soul?" (Matt. 16:26).

Our heart adheres the more intimately to one thing, the more it withdraws from others. That is why we close our eyes when we wish to concentrate. That is why in the higher regions of religion, consecrated souls leave the world to give themselves to the First Love which is the Last Love—God.

The purpose of self-discipline is to build a hierarchy. Senses are made subservient to reason, reason to faith, body to soul, and man to God.

Self-discipline requires patience. Since we do not acquire evil habits in a day, we will not break them in a day. The abuses of years may take years to rectify. "If any man will come after me, let him deny himself, and take up his cross daily, and follow me" (Luke 9:23).

The soul is made by what gets into it. Just as health depends on what we eat, so the holiness of mind depends on what we think. As we avoid poisons for the sake of the body, so we avoid evil thoughts, conversations, books, magazines, motion pictures, and companionships for the sake of the soul.

We should never let a day pass without doing three small mortifications, for example, not taking that extra cigarette or that second lump of sugar. Thus do we possess ourselves instead of being possessed by things. When these mortifications are done in the name of Our Lord, they become a source of great merit as well.

We will find God to the degree that we renounce ourselves. Some tests of knowing our nearness to God are: the patient and uncomplaining bearing of the slights and crosses of daily life; an even temper and a cheerfulness of spirit even under trying circumstances; the undertaking of all duties and legitimate pleasures and actions in the name of God and for the glory of God; a greater readiness to serve those who cannot profit us, rather than those who can.

Some motives for self-discipline are: To obtain peace of soul; to atone for one's sins; to obtain some favor or grace; to live a life more intimately with God; to conform oneself to Christ-suffering; to make reparation for the sins of others.

8

Love of Neighbor in General

There are three kinds of love. There is instinctive love, which we have in common with animals. Human beings experience it when they love not the person, but the pleasure which the person gives. The modern world calls this "sex."

The second kind of love is the distinctly human love of self-disinterestedness, which springs from an appreciation of the beauty or goodness of human nature when seen at its best. In instinctive love the good is horizontal—it refers to a good on the *same plane*.

The human love of disinterestedness is, on the contrary, vertical—it looks to a goodness on a higher plane, but still within the category of the human. It is more abstract than concrete. For example, the Philanthropist loves "humanity," the Communist his "class," the Nazi his "race," the Fascist his "nation," the Revolutionist his "cause," the soldier his "country," etc.

In each case, there is a love for an abstract "good," without any explicit reference to the source and standard of Goodness.

The third kind of love is not limited either by self-disinterestedness, nor by a high form of human goodness, but derives its inspiration from the unlimited self-giving of Divine Love which found its highest expression in Christ who died for sinners. His death was not a superlative revelation of human love, but an infinite manifestation of Divine Love; for God "spared not even his own Son" (Rom. 8:32).

Not many of us understand this third form of love because, being shut up in the circle of narrow self-interest, we can see no further than self-interest allows. We can love those who love us, and we can do good to those who do good to us, but a God who is "kind to the unthankful, and to the evil" (Luke 6:35), we fail to comprehend.

By combining the first two forms of love, one may speak of a double inspiration for fellowship. One, natural, and based on particular mutual affinities or interests—for such motives men form lodges, unions, and other organizations. The other, supernatural or divine, forbidding the claim of personal characteristics or class interests to count for anything. We are to love our fellow man not because he is lovable but because God loves him.

Brotherhood

It should be evident that the sharing of economic wealth will not make us brothers, but becoming brothers will make us share our economic wealth. The early Christians were not one because they pooled their wealth; they pooled their wealth because they were Christians.

The rich young man went to Our Lord asking: "What shall I do?" The Socialist asks: "What will *society* do?" It is man who makes society and not society which makes man. That is why all the economic schemes from Marx's Communism to the latest form of Democratic Collectivism will never unite men until they have first learned to burn, purge, and cut away their own selfishness.

The "One World" will not come at the end of an ascending line of progress, but as the resurrection from a tomb of a thousand crucified egotisms.

The reason Christianity lives and Socialist theories perish is because Socialism makes no provision for getting rid of selfishness, but Our Lord did: "Sell all whatever thou hast, and give to the poor" (Luke 18:22).

The only place in the world where Communism works is in a convent, for there the basis of having everything in common is that no one wants anything. Communism has not worked in Moscow, but it does work in a monastery.

All that economic and political revolutions do is to shift booty and loot from one party's packet to another. For that reason, none of them is really revolutionary: they all leave greed in the heart of man.

The true inspiration for fellowship is not law but love. Law is negative: "Thou shalt *not*." Love is positive: "*Love* God and *love* neighbor." Law is concerned with the minimum: "Speed limit, thirty-five miles." Love is concerned with the maximum: "Be ye therefore perfect, as also your heavenly Father is perfect" (Matt. 5:48).

Law is for moderation; love is generous: "And if a man will contend with thee in judgment, and take away thy coat, let go thy cloak also unto him. And whosoever will force thee one mile, go with him other two" (Matt. 5:40–41).

Natural generosity is limited by circumstances and relations within our own circle, and outside of these is often vindictive. Love ignores all limits, by forgiveness.

"Lord, how often shall my brother offend against me, and I forgive him? till seven times?... I say not to thee, till seven times; but till seventy times seven times" (Matt. 18:21–22). By moving from a little metaphor to a big one, Our Lord implies that precision in forgiveness is impossible. Leave it to love and it is not likely to err on the lower side.

The love of which we speak is not natural, but supernatural. By faith and good works under God's Grace, nourished by prayer and the Sacraments, we are led into intimate union with Christ—but this love we have toward Him must redound to all His creatures.

Supernatural Love

After instituting the Holy Eucharist, the night before He died, Our Lord revealed the secrets of His Heart by giving what he called a *new commandment*. "A new commandment I give unto you: That you love one another, as I have loved you, that you also love one another" (John 13:34).

Why was this precept of *charity* (for that is the proper term to describe supernatural love)—why was this precept new? Because the explicit command to love all men, regardless of race or class, or color, even though they be enemies, had never been affirmed before. From that time on, the one mark by which His followers would be known would be their supernatural love for all. "By this shall all men know that you are my disciples, if you have love one for another" (John 13:35).

On the last day, when He will come to render to every man according to his works, it will be by charity to God and to fellow man that salvation will be decided. Until the consummation of time, Christ will move through the world hidden under the guise of the needy, the poor, and the oppressed:

> Then shall the king say to them that shall be on his right hand: Come, ye blessed of my Father, possess you the kingdom prepared for you from the foundation of the world. For I was hungry, and you gave me to eat; I was thirsty, and you gave me to drink; I was a stranger, and you took me in; naked, and you covered me; sick, and you visited me; I was in prison, and you came to me.
>
> Then shall the just answer him, saying: Lord, when did we see thee hungry, and fed thee; thirsty, and gave thee drink? And when did we see thee a stranger, and took thee in? Or naked, and covered thee? Or when did we see you thee sick or in prison, and came to thee? And the king answering, shall say to them: Amen I say to you, as long as you did it to one of these my least brethren, you did it to me.
>
> Then he shall say to them also that shall be on his left hand: Depart from me, you cursed, into everlasting fire which was prepared for the devil and his angels. For I was hungry, and you gave me not to eat; I was thirsty, and you gave me not to drink; I was a stranger, and you took me not in; naked, and you covered me not; sick and in prison, and you did not visit me.
>
> Then they also shall answer him, saying: Lord, when did we see thee hungry, or thirsty, or a stranger, or naked, or sick, or in prison, and did not minister to thee?
>
> Then he shall answer them, saying: Amen I say to you, as long as you did it not to one of these least, neither did you do it to me.

> And these shall go into everlasting punishment: but the just, into life everlasting. (Matt. 25:34–46)

One of the tests of our love of God is our love of neighbor, for it is certain that we will never love our neighbor perfectly unless we love God perfectly.

It is so easy to love those of our circle, but to love those who are "below" us, or opposed to us, or "ignorant," or apparently not "worth our time," requires true spiritual insight.

> For if you love them that love you, what reward shall you have? do not even the publicans this? And if you salute your brethren only, what do you more? do not also the heathens this? Be you therefore perfect, as also your heavenly Father is perfect. (Matt. 5:46–48)

God's attitude toward us is regulated by our attitude toward our neighbor. That is why if we need something badly, the best way to *pray* for it is to give something away. If we have sinned and need forgiveness, then let us forgive our enemies. God will never be outdone by our love.

> For with what judgment you judge, you shall be judged: and with what measure you mete, it shall be measured to you again. (Matt. 7:2)

> Give and it shall be given to you: good measure and pressed down and shaken together and running over shall they give into your bosom. For with the same measure that you shall mete withal, it shall be measured to you again. (Luke 6:38)

Charity

St. Paul reminds us that charity is superior to eloquence, to prophecy, to philanthropy, to humanistic martyrdom. "If I speak with the tongues of men, and of angels, and have not charity, I am become as sounding brass, or a tinkling cymbal. And if I should have prophecy and should know all mysteries, and all knowledge, and if I should have all faith, so that I could remove mountains, and have not charity, I am nothing. And if I should distribute all my goods to feed the poor, and if I should deliver my body to be burned, and have not charity, it profiteth me nothing" (1 Cor. 13:1–3).

Charity is greater than faith, for in Heaven there will be no faith. How can one merely "believe" when one actually "sees"?

Charity is greater than hope, for there will be no hope in Heaven. How can one hope when one possesses?

But there will be charity; for God is love. "And now there remain faith, hope, and charity, these three: but the greatest of these is charity" (1 Cor. 13:13).

✠

There are nine ingredients to charity: "Charity is patient, is kind: charity envieth not, dealeth not perversely; is not puffed up; Is not ambitious, seeketh not her own, is not provoked to anger, thinketh no evil; Rejoiceth not in iniquity, but rejoiceth with the truth" (1 Cor. 13:4–6).

Patience

"Charity is patient." Charity is never in a hurry; it knocks, but breaks down no doors. A charitable heart, like the Church, knows that evil is transitory. Though evil has its "hour" as it did in the Garden of Gethsemane, God will have His "day." "But that on the good ground, are they who in a good and perfect heart, hearing the word, keep it, and bring forth fruit in patience" (Luke 8:15). "In your patience you shall possess your souls" (Luke 21:19):

> Be patient, therefore, brethren, until the coming of the Lord. Behold, the husbandman waiteth for the precious fruit of the earth: patiently bearing till he receive the early and latter rain. Be you therefore also patient, and strengthen your hearts: for the coming of the Lord is at hand. Behold, we account them blessed

> who have endured. You have heard of the patience of Job, and you have seen the end of the Lord, that the Lord is merciful and compassionate. (James 5:7, 8, 11)

Kindness

"Charity ... is kind." The whole life of Our Lord has been summarized thus: He "went about doing good" (Acts 10:38). No soul ever saves itself in isolation. We pray in the context of "*Our* Father," and live in the solidarity of the "Mystical Body of Christ." Charity is emancipation from selfishness; it is a going outside of self for the interests of others.

Although it is *kindness*, the essence of love is not *feeling*.

> My son, in thy good deeds, make no complaint, and when thou givest any thing, add not grief by an evil word. (Sir. 18:15)

> And be ye kind one to another; merciful, forgiving one another, even as God hath forgiven you in Christ. (Eph. 4:32)

Generosity

"Charity envieth not." Jealousy and envy are the tributes which mediocrity pays to genius. Charity is never competitive; it always goes beyond the limits of service or measure. When we rest on the laurels of the ordinary, we clip the wings of charity.

True generosity never looks to reciprocity; it gives neither because it expects a gift in return, nor because there is a duty or obligation to give. Charity lies beyond obligation; its essence is the "adorable extra." Its reward is in the joy of giving:

> When thou makest a dinner or a supper, call not thy friends, nor thy brethren, nor thy kinsmen, nor they neighbors who are rich; lest perhaps they also invite thee again, and a recompense be made to thee. But when thou makest a feast, call the poor, the maimed, the lame, and the blind; And thou shalt be blessed, because they

> have not wherewith to make thee recompense: for recompense shall be made thee at the resurrection of the just. (Luke 14:12–14)
>
> And if you lend to them of whom you hope to receive, what thanks are to you? For sinners also lend to sinners, for to receive as much. But love ye your enemies: do good, and lend, hoping for nothing thereby: and your reward shall be great, and you shall be the sons of the Highest; for he is kind to the unthankful, and to the evil. Be ye therefore merciful, as your Father also is merciful. (Luke 6:34–36)

Humility

"Charity is not pretentious, is not puffed up." Humility is *truth*: seeing ourselves as we really *are*; that is, as God knows our hearts. Affectation is cheating; boasting is an admission of our own indigence. Charity hides itself. The greater the vacuum there is in our heart, the more room there is for God. Full of self, empty of God:

> Thou hypocrite, cast out first the beam out of thy own eye, and then shalt thou see to cast out the mote out of thy brother's eye. (Matt. 7:5)
>
> When thou art invited to a wedding, sit not down in the first place, lest perhaps one more honourable than thou be invited by him. (Luke 14:8)
>
> Take up my yoke upon you, and learn of me, because I am meek, and humble of heart: and you shall find rest to your souls. (Matt. 11:29)

Renunciation

"Charity ... is not ambitious." The poet warned: "I charge thee, fling away ambition. By that sin fell the angels; how can man then, the image of his Maker, hope to win by it?"[8]

[8] William Shakespeare, *Henry VIII*, act 3, scene 2.

There is a rightful pursuit of the best, but what is here condemned is an insatiable lust for glory or wealth or prestige which is purchased by crawling on others' backs. "The fire never saith: It is enough" (Prov. 30:16).

Charity seeks glory, too; not the glory of men, but the glory of God. It is even willing to have its worldly position sacrificed for the advancement of truth and honor. "Blessed are ye when they shall revile you, and persecute you, and speak all that is evil against you, untruly, for my sake" (Matt. 5:11).

> It shall not be so among you, but whosoever will be the greater among you, let him be your minister: And he that will be first among you, shall be your servant. (Matt. 20:26–27)

> The kings of the Gentiles lord it over them; and they that have power over them, are called beneficent. But you not so: but he that is the greater among you, let him become as the younger; and he that is the leader, as he that serveth. For which is greater, he that sitteth at table, or he that serveth? Is it not he that sitteth at table? But I am in the midst of you, as he that serveth. (Luke 22:25–27)

> However, many of the chief men also believed in him; but because of the Pharisees they did not confess him, that they might not be cast out of the synagogue. For they loved the glory of men more than the glory of God. (John 12:42–43)

Unselfishness

"Charity . . . seeketh not her own." The way to win friends and influence people is not to flatter them, but to be selfless. The greatest happiness in life comes not from having, but from giving. From the Christian point of view, the true master is the servant.

The selfish soul who says: "I am going to do as I wish" really means "I am going to force others to do as I wish." No one loves himself too little. About the only romance some souls have is the unhappy one of loving only themselves.

The sign of the end of the world will be selfishness. "Know also this, that, in the last days, shall come dangerous times. Men shall be lovers of themselves, covetous, haughty, proud, blasphemers, disobedient to parents, ungrateful, wicked" (2 Tim. 3:1–2).

> But before all things have a constant mutual charity among yourselves: for charity covereth a multitude of sins. (1 Pet. 4:8)

> And that he should be loved with the whole heart, and with the whole understanding, and with the whole soul, and with the whole strength; and to love one's neighbour as one's self, is a greater thing than all holocausts and sacrifices. (Mark 12:33)

> See thou never do to another what thou wouldst hate to have done to thee by another. (Tob. 4:16)

> Greater love than this no man hath, that a man lay down his life for his friends. (John 15:13)

> For God so loved the world, as to give his only begotten Son; that whosoever believeth in him, may not perish, but may have life everlasting. (John 3:16)

> Bear ye one another's burdens; and so you shall fulfill the law of Christ. (Gal. 6:2)

Good Temper

"Charity … is not provoked to anger." Bad temper is an indication of a man's character; every man can be judged by the things which make him mad. Heaven could be ruined by one single soul who was *touchy*. "A peaceable tongue is a tree of life: but that which is immoderate, shall crush the spirit" (Prov. 15:4). "A hot soul is a burning fire, it will never be quenched, till it devour some thing" (Sir. 23:22).

The way to sweeten a soul is not just to take hate out, but to put love in. The even-tempered man possesses his soul. He never flies into a rage at others because he knows that God might rightfully be angry with him. By practicing good-naturedness with others, he hopes to obtain the blessing of God on himself.

Our Lord did not throw stones back at those who would have taken His life. "They took up stones therefore to cast at him. But Jesus hid himself, and went out of the temple" (John 8:59).

> A mild answer breaketh wrath, but a harsh word stirreth up fury. (Prov. 15:1)

> Brethren, and if a man be overtaken in any fault, you, who are spiritual, instruct such a one in the spirit of meekness, considering thyself, lest thou also be tempted. (Gal. 6:1)

> But the servant of the Lord must not wrangle: but be mild towards all men, apt to teach, patient. (2 Tim. 2:24)

Guilelessness

"Charity . . . thinketh no evil." Those who most readily attribute evil to others are generally themselves evil. A dishonest politician will invariably accuse all politicians of being dishonest; an unfaithful husband will accuse his wife of infidelity.

The sense of justice is so deep-rooted in us that if we are not good, we try to pacify our consciences by attributing the same evil to others. Charity, on the contrary, is unsuspicious; and, because it believes in others, is most encouraging of good. Charity never imputes the evil motive, never judges solely by externals:

> Whosoever speaketh ill of any thing, bindeth himself for the time to come: but he that feareth the commandment, shall dwell in peace. (Prov. 13:13)

> But do not apply thy heart to all words that are spoken: lest perhaps thou hear thy servant reviling thee. For thy conscience knoweth that thou also hast often spoken evil of others. (Eccles. 7:22–23)

> For our glory is this, the testimony of our conscience, that in simplicity of heart and sincerity of God, and not in carnal wisdom, but in the grace of God, we have conversed in this world: and more abundantly towards you. (2 Cor. 1:12)

> Purifying your souls in the obedience of charity, with a brotherly love, from a sincere heart love one another earnestly. (1 Pet. 1:22)

> That you may be blameless, and sincere children of God, without reproof, in the midst of a crooked and perverse generation; among whom you shine as lights in the world. (Phil. 2:15)

Sincerity

"Charity rejoiceth not in iniquity, but rejoiceth with the truth." It is a common human standard to judge virtues by the vices from which we abstain; and to find the wickedness of others an excuse for our own: "I am just as good as the next fellow."

Charity, on the contrary, refuses to capitalize on others' failings. Its joy is found in truth, and in things as they really are. Charity refuses to subscribe to the modem dictum that "good and evil depend entirely on your subjective point of view." *In truth* means independent of self.

> Woe to you that call evil good, and good evil: that put darkness for light, and light for darkness: that put bitter for sweet, and sweet for bitter. (Isa. 5:20)

> Why art thou seduced, my son, by a strange woman, and art cherished in the bosom of another? (Prov. 5:20)

> Rejoice in the Lord always; again, I say, rejoice. (Phil. 4:4)

> The kingdom of heaven is like unto a treasure hidden in a field. Which a man having found, hid it, and for joy thereof goeth, and selleth all that he hath, and buyeth that field. (Matt. 13:44)

> Delight in the Lord, and he will give thee the requests of thy heart. (Ps. 36:4)

> So also you now indeed have sorrow; but I will see you again, and your heart shall rejoice; and your joy no man shall take from you. (John 16:22)

Physical and Spiritual Expressions of Charity

There are seven ways in which charity may be expressed physically:

- to feed the hungry
- to give drink to the thirsty
- to clothe the naked
- to succor the stranger
- to visit the sick
- to ransom the captive
- to bury the dead

There are seven ways in which charity may be expressed spiritually:

- to instruct the ignorant
- to counsel the doubtful
- to admonish sinners
- to bear wrongs patiently
- to forgive offenses willingly
- to comfort the afflicted
- to pray for the living and the dead

9

Friendship of Christians with Jews

Our Christian faith is like a grafted branch that grows out from the roots of the Olive Tree of Israel. Shall Christians delay the day of the fellowship of all men in God, by hatred of a people from whom salvation came as from a root?

"For if the firstfruit be holy, so is the lump also: and if the root be holy, so are the branches. And if some of the branches be broken, and thou, being a wild olive, art ingrafted in them, and art made partaker of the root, and of the fatness of the olive tree, Boast not against the branches. But if thou boast, thou bearest not the root, but the root thee.... Be not highminded, but fear. For if God hath not spared the natural branches, fear lest perhaps he also spare not thee" (Rom. 11:16–18, 20–21).

For a Catholic, to be anti-Semitic is to be un-Catholic.

Pope Pius XI, commenting on the words in the Canon of the Mass—"sacrificium Patriarchae nostri Abrahae," the sacrifice of our father Abraham—said, "Notice that Abraham is called our Patriarch, our ancestor. Anti-Semitism is incompatible with the thought and the sublime reality expressed in this text. It is a movement in which we Christians can have no part whatsoever.... Anti-Semitism is unacceptable. Spiritually we are Semites."[9]

9 Pius XI, Allocution to Directors of the Belgian Catholic Radio Agency (September 1938), quoted in Jacques Maritain, *Anti-Semitism* (London: Centenary Press, 1939), 27.

There are many lies told against the Jews. One of them is *The Protocols of the Elders of Zion* which inspires so much anti-Semitism. It supposedly contains an elaborate war plan for the attainment of world dominion through Jewish Freemasons' Lodges.

This work is a forgery. It appeared for the first time in a book written by a certain Russian anti-Semite, Sergius Nilus, entitled *The Great within the Small*, which revealed the anti-Christ as a near political possibility.

The fact is Nilius plagiarized these ideas from the work of a French lawyer, Maurice Joly, *Dialogues in Hell*, published in 1865—with this principal difference: Joly made Napoleon the one who sought world domination. Nilius changed Napoleon III to the Jews and so the lie was born.

What would Christianity be without Jesus who came to the world from Israel?

What would the Church be without the twelve Jews who were Apostles of the Messiah?

What would Christianity be without the background of Abraham, Moses, Isaac, John the Baptist, and the prophets who announced the Messiah?

Did not Our Lord Himself say: "Do not think that I am come to destroy the law, or the prophets. I am not come to destroy, but to fulfill. For amen, I say unto you, till heaven and earth pass, one jot, or one tittle shall not pass of the law, till all be fulfilled" (Matt. 5:17–18)?

Did not Philip cry out to Nathaniel when they saw Jesus: "We have found him of whom Moses in the law, and the prophets did write, Jesus the son of Joseph of Nazareth" (John 1:45)?

The promise of a Savior was made to the Jews, not to the Gentiles.

A Christian may attempt to justify his anti-Semitism on the ground that the Jews are hated by the world. Shall the Christian forget that if he were a real Christian, he, too, would be hated by the world: "I have chosen you out of the world, therefore the world hateth you" (John 15:19)?

An anti-Semite seeks to justify his hatred on the ground that the Jews are our enemies. Even if they were, is not a Christian supposed to love his enemies? "Love your enemies: do good to them that hate you: and pray for them that persecute and calumniate you: That you may be the children of your Father who is in heaven, who maketh his sun to rise upon the good, and bad, and raineth upon the just and the unjust." (Matt. 5:44–45)

Few people on the face of the earth suffered as much in recent years as the Jews. Shall Christians despise them who through suffering have become more like our Master than they themselves become through their hate and criticism?

Our Blessed Lord in the story of the Good Samaritan told the Jew to love his neighbor—who, in that particular instance, was a despised alien and half-breed. The Jew today is my neighbor. I may not hate him whom Christ ordered me to love.

How does the Christian ever expect the Jew to accept the Christian code unless he, the Christian, acts like a Christian? Hating the Jew will do more harm to the Christian soul than it will ever do to the Jew.

If a Christian loves the land that was sanctified by the feet of the Savior, he ought also to love the people from whom came His Christ, the Savior of the world.

On September 25, 1928, the decree of the Holy Office stated: "The Catholic Church habitually prays for the Jewish people who were the bearers of the divine revelation up to the time of Christ; this, despite, indeed, on account of, their subsequent blindness. Actuated by this love, the Apostolic See has protected this people against unjust oppression and, just as every kind of envy and jealousy among the nations must be disapproved of, so in an *especial manner* must be that hatred which is generally termed anti-Semitism."[10]

The Jews are to be no exceptions to the words of Our Lord: "All things therefore whatsoever you would that men should do to you, do you also to them. For this is the law and the prophets" (Matt. 7:12).

The disintegration of Christianity is not to be laid at the door of the Jews. Those who had most influence in robbing minds of the Divinity of

[10] Quoted in Catholic European Scholars, *The Church and the Jews: A Memorial*, ed. Gregory Feige (New York: Catholic Association for International Peace, Paulist Press, 1937), 16.

Christ, by ridicule, slander, or by denying His existence, were not Jews: Voltaire, Rousseau, Hume, Kant, Hegel, Schleiermacher, Schopenhauer, Feuerbach, Friedrich Strauss, Nietzsche, Buechner, Haeckel, Drews, and the thousand lesser lights of today.

Anti-Semitism is anti-Christianity.

If a Jew has violated any of the laws of the State, the State may punish him for having done so; but the State may not do so simply because he is a Jew.

Germany did not become more Christian, more moral, and more human after its elimination of the Jews.

> I am a Jew. Hath not a Jew eyes?
> Hath not a Jew hands, organs, dimensions,
> senses, affections, passions?
> fed with the same food, hurt with the
> same weapons, subject to the same
> diseases, healed by the same means,
> warmed and cooled by the same winter
> and summer as a Christian is?[11]

[11] William Shakespeare, *The Merchant of Venice*, act 3, scene 1.

10

Friendship of Jews with Christians

Dr. Cecil Roth, Jewish historian, addressing the Zionist Forum in Buffalo, New York, February 25, 1937, said: "We Jews who have suffered so much from prejudices, should rid our minds of prejudices and learn the facts. The truth is that the Popes and the Catholic Church from the earliest days of the Church were never responsible for physical persecution of Jews, and only Rome, among the capitals of the world, is free from having been a place of Jewish tragedy. For this, we Jews must have gratitude."

A Jew knows that anti-Semitism is not due to Christianity, because he knows that his people were persecuted before the advent of Christianity.

A Jew will never say that a child in a Catholic School or Protestant Sunday School is taught "to hate the Jews because they crucified Christ." The fact is each child is taught to beat his own breast, and to accuse himself, because *his sins* were the cause of that Crucifixion.

The primary meaning of the crucifix to every Christian is: *I* sold the Lord; *I* betrayed Him; *I* crucified Him. "Now when you sin thus against the brethren, and wound their weak conscience, you sin against Christ" (1 Cor. 8:12).

No Christian hates the Jews because of the Crucifixion related in the Gospels—any more than the British hate the Americans because of the Declaration of Independence.

A Jew knows it is just as unreasonable to say the Christian is made to hate the Jew whenever the Christian speaks of Calvary, as it is to say that Americans are told to hate the English whenever Americans sing "The Star-Spangled Banner."

A Jew knows that a good Christian is taught to love his neighbor and to love his enemies. Whenever therefore he falls from that ideal, and hates his fellowman, it is not because he is Christian, but because *he is not.*

A Jew knows that today all religions are persecuted. No race and no faith has a monopoly on persecution. Protestants have been persecuted in Germany, and Catholics, like the Jews, have been persecuted in every age.

No one has a right to talk on the subject of persecution unless he condemns it wherever he finds it, and irrespective of who is persecuted, whether it be a Jew, a Protestant, or a Catholic. Persecution is not essentially anti-Semitic, it is not essentially anti-Christian. It is anti-human.

Over-sensitiveness is a great barrier to friendly relations. Not every Jew is a saint and not every Christian is Christ-like. If then a Christian deplores that a particular Jew publishes filthy books disruptive of morality, the Jews must not accuse the Christian of being anti-Semitic; and because a Jew deplores the social or political injustice of a particular Christian, the Christians must not retort that the Jew is anti-Christian, or a Communist.

Christianity cannot be anti-Semitic, because it honors such Jews as Abraham, Isaac, Jacob, Moses, David. Were not the twelve Apostles Jews? Was not the first Pope a Jew? Does not the Church use the Old Testament as much as the Synagogue does? Have not its scholars defended the authenticity of the Old Testament?

> The hatred of the Jews and the hatred of the Christians springs from a common source, from the same recalcitrance of the world, which desires to be wounded ... neither with the wounds of Israel for its movement in time, nor by the Cross of Jesus for eternal life.[12]

[12] Jacques Maritain, *A Christian Looks at the Jewish Question* (New York: Longmans, Green and Company, 1939), 30.

The Jew and the Christian begin to hate one another at that moment when both look for *external* causes of their misery, the Jew putting all the blame on the Christian story of the Crucifixion, and the Christian putting all the blame on the Jews.

The Jew and the Christian begin to love one another when both look for the *internal* causes of their misery; that is, their sins and their forgetfulness of the moral law of God.

There is no Jew in the world who loves God and hates Christians, and there is no Christian in the world who truly loves God-made-man and hates Jews. Anti-Christianity and anti-Semitism are the yardsticks of our mutual failure to be religious.

Someday we hope to see a parade with the Jews carrying banners protesting against the persecution of Christians, and Christians carrying banners protesting against the persecution of the Jews.

The glory of the Jews is the Law they received from God. The greatest bond of unity between Jews and Christians is the keeping of the commandments of God:

> I am the Lord thy God, who brought thee out of the land of Egypt, out of the house of bondage. Thou shalt not have strange gods before me....
>
> Thou shalt not take the name of the Lord thy God in vain: for the Lord will not hold him guiltless that shall take the name of the Lord his God in vain.
>
> Remember that thou keep holy the sabbath day....
>
> Honor thy father and thy mother, that thou mayest be longlived upon the land which the Lord thy God will give thee.
>
> Thou shalt not kill.
>
> Thou shalt not commit adultery.
>
> Thou shalt not steal.
>
> Thou shalt not bear false witness against thy neighbour.
>
> Thou shalt not covet thy neighbour's house: neither shalt thou desire his wife, nor his servant, nor his handmaid, nor his ox, nor his ass, nor any thing that is his. (Exod. 20:2–3, 7–8, 12–17).

11

Friendship of Catholics with Protestants

Protestantism began a little over four hundred years ago. A reformation was needed. Not the reformation of *faith* which disrupted Christian unity, but a reformation of *morals* which the Church initiated at the Council of Trent.

It would therefore be well for Catholics to recall the warning words of Cardinal Pole delivered during those trying times: "We may wish to deny that we have given birth to these heresies which are everywhere rife, because we ourselves have not uttered any heresy. Nevertheless, if we have not tilled our field as we ought—if we have not sowed—if we took no pains at once to root up the springing weeds—we are no less to be reckoned their cause than if we ourselves had sowed them.... Because the salt has lost its savor we are suffering justly, yet not for the sake of justice."[13]

The best attitude a Catholic can take to a Protestant is to live up to the spiritual life of the Church, that non-Catholics seeing Christ reflected in their lives may desire to see that happiness fulfilled in them.

When men are starving you need not tell them to avoid poison, nor even to eat bread. One need only give nourishment and the laws of life

[13] Cardinal Reginald Pole, Legatine Address at the second session of the Council of Trent, January 7, 1546.

will do the rest. In the religious sphere, in like manner, it is wrong to concentrate exclusively on pointing out errors. It is better to speak of the fullness of the life of Christ, and the grace of God will do the rest.

Be not more Catholic than the Church, for the Church does not call all Protestants formal "heretics." If their ignorance is morally invincible, they are not to be called heretics or guilty in the eyes of God, says the official teaching of the Church.

Leo XIII, in a letter to the Episcopalian Archbishops of Canterbury and York, wrote: "We indeed allow that those who are separated from Catholic unity, and have been imbued with other doctrines from their youth up, may be sincere and in good faith, so long as the truth is not suitably or sufficiently set clear to them. The one judge of the secrets of hearts is God."

The Church officially calls those not of the faith "our separated brethren."

The bad Catholic who gives no glory to God, and offends Him, is heading for eternal loss. The non-Catholic who gives glory to God, according to the light of his conscience, is in his way to be saved. It ill-behooves a Catholic to act like the elder son when the prodigal came home. God is more anxious to see all His sheep in "one fold" than we are (see John 10:16).

A Catholic must be very intolerant about the truths of His Faith, for the truths are God's and he has no rights over them. But he must be very tolerant to those who do not share that truth, for God is the judge of hearts.

> Far be it from the members of the Catholic Church to exhibit any enmity in any way towards [strangers to the true faith and Catholic unity through no fault of their own]. Rather let them fulfill all the duties of Christian Charity towards them, above all to the poor, the sick, and those afflicted in any way amongst them.[14]

[14] Pius IX, encyclical letter *Quanto conficiamur moerore* (August 10, 1863), 9, quoted in Frs. Rumble and Carty, *Radio Replies*, vol. 3 (Charlotte, N.C.: TAN Books, 2012), 1044.

No Catholic may rejoice at the vast increase in religious indifference. It is never permitted to wish that what we believe to be impoverished should be impoverished still more. If a man were hungry, would we want him to die of hunger? Any decline in the belief of the Doctrine of Christ among our separated brethren is to some extent a loss to the Church, and to the world.

If we Catholics believed all the lies and calumnies that are told about the Church, we would hate it ten times more than bigots do. The enemies of the Church often do not hate the Church: they only hate what they erroneously believe to be the Church.

Catholics often make the great mistake of believing that they are right because of their superior understanding. No! If they enjoy the fullness of faith it is because of a gift of God.

On the other hand, Catholics may erroneously believe that others are wrong through their own fault. No! Many of them are living up to the dictates of their consciences as they see the light.

There is no religion on the face of God's earth that does not possess some truth. Instead of concentrating on error, Catholics should take hold of that segment of truth and complete the circle by revealing the fullness of the Truth and Love of Christ.

Chesterton once said that no Protestant could ever keep him out of the Catholic Church. Only a bad Catholic who gave scandal could do it.[15]

No Catholic may ever compromise a single truth of His Church, for Truth is of God's making, not ours. But though he is as intolerant about Christ's Truth as he is about two and two making four, he must be tolerant, kind, and charitable to all persons who do not share his faith, or are even opposed to it. The foundation of Catholic tolerance is not indifference to truth, but Faith, Hope, and Charity.

We have been sent into the world not to condemn, but through love to bring all men to Christ.

[15] See G.K. Chesterton, *The Catholic Church and Conversion* (San Francisco: Ignatius, 2006), in chap. 3, "The Real Obstacles."

No bigot is to be regarded as beyond conversion. St. Paul was a bigot. No sinner is to be regarded as too vile for union with Our Lord. Mary Magdalen was a sinner.

"By these shall all men know that you are my disciples, if you have love one for another" (John 13:35).

12

Friendship of Non-Catholics with Catholics

Judge the Catholic Church not by those who barely live by its spirit, but by the example of those who live closest to it. Art is best known through its highest representatives, not through those who daub.

The correct definition of a good Catholic is a Catholic who takes the salvation of his soul seriously.

A Catholic believes that religion is not only individual but social; that the individual receives his religion from the spiritual community or the Church, and not the other way around. It is not the union of individual believers which makes a Church; it is the Church which begets, sustains, and nourishes the individual believer.

A Catholic believes that the common life of religion is not a human fellowship, but is a fellowship of consecrated persons.

This fellowship is both vertical and horizontal; vertical because God is its Author, horizontal because it embraces all men who are "partakers of the Divine Life" (see 2 Pet. 1:4).

In other words, fellowship with man is impossible without fellowship with God. Men cannot be brothers unless they have God as their common father, and God is not a Father unless He has a Son, according to Whose Image we are made and in Whose Spirit we are quickened and united.

A Catholic believes that what the world calls "charity," or material kindness to neighbor, does not really become charity until self-giving to the brethren is based on the self-giving of God to us; for that reason, it is a direct product of His Grace.

"Therefore, whether you eat or drink, or whatsoever else you do, do all for the glory of God" (1 Cor. 10:31). "For you know the grace of our Lord Jesus Christ, that being rich he became poor, for your sakes; that through his poverty you might be rich" (2 Cor. 8:9).

A Catholic believes that the Church is not an institution but a life; that it was not formed from the outside in, by Our Lord calling men together to form an organization, but from the inside out, by Our Lord sending His Spirit and thus making them one because they had one soul, the Holy Spirit.

A Catholic believes that, since his Church is Christ-made, it may not be man-unmade. He believes, too, that it never suits the particular mood of any age, because it was made for all ages.

A Catholic knows that if the Church married the mood of any age in which it lived, it would be a widow in the next age. The mark of the true Church is that it will never get on well with the passing moods of the world: "I have chosen you out of the world, therefore the world hateth you" (John 15:19).

The normal adult approach to the Catholic religion does not begin with faith, but with reason and history. What credit is to business, that faith is to a Catholic. There must be a reason for extending credit and there must be a reason for faith. Hence St. Peter said: "But sanctify the Lord Christ in your hearts, being ready always to satisfy every one that asketh you a reason of that hope which is in you" (1 Pet. 3:15).

A Catholic may sin as badly as anyone else, but no genuine Catholic ever denies he is a sinner. A Catholic wants his sins forgiven—not excused or sublimated.

A Catholic believes that Our Lord is present in the Eucharist in every Catholic church. That is why he tips his hat when he passes a church. That is why he genuflects when he enters the church. That is why there are kneeling benches in church; for adoration is physically expressed by the humility of kneeling.

A Catholic believes that the only true progress in the world consists in the diminution of the traces of Original Sin.

A Catholic believes that remarriage after divorce and artificial birth control are wrong, not simply because the Church has so decreed, but because these practices are opposed to the natural law and to the supernatural law of Christ.

Catholics build their own schools, while paying taxes for non-religious schools, because they want their children to be educated in the love of Christ and His moral law, and thus to save their souls and become worthy citizens of their country.

A Catholic does not believe that man can forgive sins, but he does believe that God can forgive sins *through man*. Christ communicated to His Church: "Whose sins you shall forgive, they are forgiven them; and whose sins you shall retain, they are retained" (John 20:23).

13

Friendship with All Peoples, Races, Classes, and Colors

In every single instance, hatred against any person is, at bottom, a *want* of religion.

Hatred of one's fellowman is an impediment to friendship with God. Love of God and of neighbor are inseparable. "If therefore thou offer thy gift at the altar, and there thou remember that thy brother hath anything against thee; Leave there thy offering before the altar, and go first to be reconciled to thy brother: and then coming thou shalt offer thy gift" (Matt. 5:23–24).

Our Blessed Lord in His preaching canceled all snobberies of race and blood and color. When His Mother and relatives came to seek Him, He looked at them and said: "Behold my mother and my brethren. For whosoever shall do the will of my Father, that is in heaven, he is my brother, and sister, and mother" (Matt. 12:49–50). From that point on the new relationship between men was to be grounded on the will of God.

We will never regard all our fellow men as brothers until we recognize God as our Father: Humanism is dying because it has severed its affection for humanity from its roots which are in God.

The true Christian will see Our Lord's Incarnation prolonged in every human need: "I was in prison and you visited me" (see Matt. 25:36). Touch any human being in the world—anyone, whether he be a Communist, a

Mohammedan, a Negro, a Buddhist, a Japanese—and you touch a person for whom Christ died, even though he knows it not.

One day, the enemies of Our Lord came to Him and said, "Master, we know that thou speakest and teachest rightly: and thou dost not respect any person, but teachest the way of God in truth" (Luke 20:21). Even his enemies recognized that fundamental principle of His teaching—the sovereign worth of every person in the world. Karl Marx said an individual man had no value unless he belonged to the revolutionary class. Our Lord said a man had a value regardless of his class. "Thus therefore shall you pray: *Our* Father who art in heaven" (Matt. 6:9; emphasis added).

Standing on the Hill of Mars dedicated to the god of war, St. Paul announced to the Greeks, who felt themselves superior: "God ... made the world, and all things therein; he, being Lord of heaven ... hath made of one, all mankind, to dwell upon the whole face of the earth, determining appointed times, and the limits of their habitation" (Acts 17:24, 26).

Blood transfusions prove that though there are four types of blood, it makes absolutely no difference from what race or color the blood be taken, so long as it is the right type.

In the new creation of Divine Grace:

- *There are no racial distinctions*: "There is neither Gentile nor Jew" (Col. 3:11).
- *No physical distinction*: There is neither "circumcision nor uncircumcision" (Col. 3:11).
- *No cultural distinction*: There is neither "Barbarian nor Scythian" (Col. 3:11).
- *No social distinction*: There is neither "bond nor free" (Col. 3:11).
- "*But Christ is all, and in all*" (Col. 3:11; emphasis added).

The accidents of life, such as political position, wealth, education, are not occasions for pride, but opportunities for service: "To reveal his Son in me, that I might preach him among the Gentiles, immediately I condescended not to flesh and blood" (Gal. 1:16).

When a slave, Onesimus, came to St. Paul and was converted, Paul sent him back to his owner, Philemon, with the reminder that he was no longer a slave, but a brother through sharing Christ's grace: "Not now as a servant, but instead of a servant, a most dear brother, especially to me: but how much more to thee both in the flesh and in the Lord?" (Philem. 1:16).

Is it any wonder that Nietzsche, who hated Christ, should write: "Christianity has waged a deadly war ... [against the] distance between man and man.... And if belief in the 'privileges of the majority' makes and *will continue to make* revolutions—it is Christianity [which is responsible].... Christianity is a revolt of all creatures that creep on the ground against everything that is *lofty*."[16]

The basic reason why Communism is wrong is because it insists on the privilege of class; Nazism is wrong because it insists on the privilege of race; Fascism is wrong because it insists on the privilege of nation. Hence in theory all are anti-Christian. Think of what a revolution Christianity can be to India if the sixty million untouchables find themselves capable of becoming "children of God and heirs of Heaven" (see Rom. 8:17).

Because every person is either potentially or actually a child of God, reverence must be shown to every human being in the world:

- *Reverence for those whom we regard as inferior* and whom we ridicule as fools because they are not of our race or class or color: "But I say to you, that whosoever is angry with his brother, shall be in danger of the judgment. And whosoever shall say to his brother, Raca, shall be in danger of the council. And whosoever shall say, Thou fool, shall be in danger of hell fire" (Matt. 5:22).
- *Reverence for women*: "You have heard that it was said to them of old: Thou shalt not commit adultery. But I say to you, that whosoever shall look on a woman to lust after her, hath already committed adultery with her in his heart" (Matt. 5:27–28).
- *Reverence for the purity of our own mind and heart*: "And if thy right eye scandalize thee, pluck it out and cast it from thee. For it is expedient for thee that one of thy members should perish, rather

[16] Friedrich Nietzsche, *The Antichrist*, vol. 18 in *The Complete Works of Friedrich Nietzsche* (Hastings, U.K.: Delphia Classics, 2017), 43.

than that thy whole body be cast into hell. And if thy right hand scandalize thee, cut it off, and cast it from thee: for it is expedient for thee that one of thy members should perish, rather than that thy whole body be cast into hell" (Matt. 5:29–30).

- *Reverence for wife*: In vain will men expect nations to keep international treaties, if they break domestic treaties: "What therefore God hath joined together, let no man put asunder" (Matt. 19:6). "But I say to you, that whosoever shall put away his wife, excepting for the cause of fornication, maketh her to commit adultery: and he that shall marry her that is put away, committeth adultery" (Matt. 5:32).
- *Reverence for peace*: "You have heard that it hath been said, An eye for an eye, and a tooth for a tooth. But I say to you not to resist evil: but if one strike thee on thy right cheek, turn to him also the other" (Matt. 5:38–39).
- *Reverence for those who have a right to command*: "Servants, be obedient to them that are your lords according to the flesh, with fear and trembling, in the simplicity of your heart, as to Christ" (Eph. 6:5).
- *Reverence for the needy*: "Give to him that asketh of thee and from him that would borrow of thee turn not away" (Matt. 5:42).
- *Reverence for enemies*: "You have heard that it hath been said, Thou shalt love thy neighbour, and hate thy enemy. But I say to you, Love your enemies: do good to them that hate you: and pray for them that persecute and calumniate you: That you may be the children of your Father who is in heaven, who maketh his sun to rise upon the good, and bad, and raineth upon the just and the unjust" (Matt. 5:43–45).

The fingers of others which we refuse to grasp in handshake will on the Day of Judgment bar our way into the Kingdom of Heaven.

True Christian greatness is measured not by superiority, but by service: "And he that will be first among you, shall be your servant" (Matt. 20:27). The greatest race on earth is the race that renders the most service to others in the name of God.

To one who hated his people that great Colored leader Booker Washington once said: "I resolved that I would no longer let any man narrow and degrade my soul ... by causing me to hate him."[17] There is a truly Christian resolution.

> And they sung a new canticle, saying: Thou art worthy, O Lord, to take the book, and to open the seals thereof; because thou wast slain, and hast redeemed us to God, in thy blood, out of every tribe, and tongue, and people, and nation. And hast made us to our God a kingdom and priests, and we shall reign on the earth. (Rev. 5:9–10)

> Who would imagine as we see [men] thus filled with hatred of one another, that they are all of one common stock, all of the same nature, all members of the same human society? Who would recognize brothers, whose Father is in Heaven?[18]

> We confess that We feel a special paternal affection, which is certainly inspired of Heaven, for the Negro people dwelling among you; for in the field of religion and education We know that they need special care and comfort and are very deserving of it. We therefore invoke an abundance of heavenly blessing and We pray fruitful success for those whose generous zeal is devoted to their welfare.[19]

[17] Quoted in John J. Ansbro, *The Credos of Eight Black Leaders: Converting Obstacles into Opportunities* (Lanham, MD: University Press, 2004), 27.

[18] Benedict XV, encyclical letter *Ad beatissimi apostolorum* (November 1, 1914), 3.

[19] Pius XII, encyclical letter *Sertum laetitiae* (November 1, 1939), 9.

14

Necessary Basis of Love of Neighbor: Love of God

The solution of the problem of tolerance is not the carrying on of anti-hate campaigns, for unless there is love, how can hate be abolished; nor by interpreting tolerance as indifference to truth and by whittling down God's revelation to fit those who no longer believe in revelation. The discords and hates among classes and races and creeds can be sublimated and abolished only by a love of God. In order to cultivate that love of God, we invoke the appeal of those who know something about it to encourage us in the art of Divine Friendship:

> Abide in me, and I in you. As the branch cannot bear fruit of itself, unless it abide in the vine, so neither can you, unless you abide in me. I am the vine; you the branches: he that abideth in me, and I in him, the same beareth much fruit: for without me you can do nothing....
>
> As the Father hath loved me, I also have loved you. Abide in my love. If you keep my commandments, you shall abide in my love; as I also have kept my Father's commandments, and do abide in his love.... You are my friends, if you do the things that I command you....
>
> These things I command you, that you love one another. If the world hate you, know ye, that it hath hated me before you. If you

had been of the world, the world would love its own: but because you are not of the world, but I have chosen you out of the world, therefore the world hateth you.

Remember my word that I said to you: The servant is not greater than his master. If they have persecuted me, they will also persecute you: if they have kept my word, they will keep yours also. (John 15:4–5, 9–10, 14, 17–20)

✠

These things Jesus spoke, and lifting up his eyes to heaven, he said: Father, the hour is come, glorify thy Son, that thy Son may glorify thee.... I pray not that thou shouldst take them out of the world, but that thou shouldst keep them from evil. They are not of the world, as I also am not of the world. Sanctify them in the truth. Thy word is truth. As thou hast sent me into the world, I also have sent them into the world. And for them do I sanctify myself, that they also may be sanctified in truth.

And not for them only do I pray, but for them also who through their word shall believe in me; that they all may be one, as thou, Father, in me, and I in thee; that they also may be one in us; that the world may believe that thou has sent me.

And the glory which thou hast given me, I have given to them; that they may be one, as we also are one: I in them, and thou in me; that they may be made perfect in one: and the world may know that thou hast sent me, and hast loved them, as thou hast also loved me.... And I have made known thy name to them, and will make it known, that the love wherewith thou hast loved me, may be in them, and I in them. (John 17:1, 15–23, 26)

✠

Who then shall separate us from the love of Christ? Shall tribulation? or distress? or famine? or nakedness? or danger? or persecution? or the sword? (As it is written: For thy sake, we are put to death all the day long. We are accounted as sheep for the slaughter.) But in all these things we overcome, because of him that hath loved us. For I am sure that neither death, nor life, nor angels, nor principalities, nor powers, nor things present, nor things to come, nor might, nor height, nor depth, nor any other creature, shall be able to separate us from the love of God, which is in Christ Jesus our Lord. (Rom. 8:35–39)

But flesh and blood, this vessel of clay, this earthen dwelling place, when shall it attain at last to . . . [love]? When shall it feel affection like this, so that inebriated with Divine Love, forgetful of self, and become to itself like a broken vessel, it may utterly pass over into God, and so adhere to Him as to become one spirit with Him?. . .

Blessed and holy should I call that man to whom it has been granted to experience such a thing in this mortal life, were it *only* rarely, or even but once, and this, so to speak, in passing, and for the space of a moment. For, in a certain manner to lose thyself, as though thou wert not, and to be utterly unconscious of thyself, and to be emptied of thyself, and brought almost to nothing . . . that pertains to the life of Heaven and not to the life of human affection.

And if indeed any mortal is occasionally admitted to this, in passing, as I have said, and only for a moment, then straightway the wicked world begins to envy him, and the evil of the day disturbs, this body of death becomes a burden, the necessity of flesh provokes, the weakness of the corruption does not endure it, and what is even more insistent than these, fraternal charity recalls.

Alas! he is compelled to return into himself, to fall back into his own and miserably to exclaim: "Lord, I suffer violence, do Thou answer for me"; and this "Unhappy man that I am, who shall deliver me from the body of this death?"

Nevertheless, since the Scripture saith that God hath made all things for Himself (Prov. 16:4) the creature will surely at some time confirm itself and bring itself into harmony with its author.

Some day then we shall come to love as He loves; so that even as God willed all things to exist only for Himself, so we too may will to have been and to be, neither ourselves nor naught else save equally for His sake, to serve His Will alone, and not our pleasure.

Truly, not the appeasing of our necessity, nor the obtaining of felicity will delight us so much as that His Will shall be fulfilled in us and concerning us; which to we daily ask in our prayer when we say: Thy Will be done on earth as it is in heaven.

O, holy and chaste love! O sweet and tender affection! O pure and perfect intention of the will . . . surely so much the more perfect and pure as there is in it nothing now mixed of its own, the more sweet and tender as naught is felt but what is divine. Thus to be affected is to become Godlike.[20]

✠

The soul then, being thus inwardly recollected, in God or before God, now and then becomes so sweetly attentive to the goodness of the well-beloved, that her attention seems not to be attention, so purely and delicately is it exercised: as it happens to certain rivers, which glide so calmly and smoothly that beholders, and such as float upon them, seem neither to see nor feel any motion, because the waters are not seen to ripple or flow at all. . . .

Even human lovers are content, sometimes, with being near or within sight of the person they love without speaking to her, and without even distinctly thinking of her or her perfections, satiated, as it were, and satisfied to relish this dear presence, not by any reflection they make upon it, but by a certain gratification and repose which their spirit takes in it. . . .

Now this repose sometimes goes so deep in its tranquillity, that the whole soul and all its powers fall as it were asleep, and make

[20] St. Bernard of Clairvaux, *De deligendo Deo*, 10.

no movement nor action whatever, except the will alone, and even this does no more than receive the delight and satisfaction which the presence of the well-beloved affords.

And what is yet more admirable is, that the will does not even perceive the delight and contentment which she receives, enjoying it insensibly, being not mindful of herself but of Him whose presence gives her this pleasure, as happens frequently when, surprised by a light slumber, we only hear indistinctly what our friends are saying around us, or feel their caresses almost imperceptibly, not feeling that we feel.[21]

✠

What a man cannot amend in himself or others, he must bear with patience, till God ordains otherwise.

Think that perhaps it is better so for thy trial and patience; without which our merits are of little worth.

Thou must, nevertheless, under such impediments, earnestly pray that God may vouchsafe to help thee, and that thou mayest bear them well.

If any one, being once or twice admonished, does not comply, contend not with him; but commit all to God, that His will may be done, and that He may be honoured in all His servants, who knows how to convert evil into good.

Endeavour to be patient in supporting the defects and infirmities of others, of what kind soever; because thou also hast many things which others must bear withal.

If thou canst not make thyself such a one as thou wouldst, how canst thou expect to have another according to thy liking?

We would willingly have others perfect; and yet we mend not our own defects.

[21] St. Francis de Sales, "On the Repose of a Soul Recollected in Her Well-Beloved," chap. 8 in *Treatise on the Love of God*, trans. Dom Henry Benedict Mackey, O.S.B. (Charlotte, NC: TAN Books, 2012).

We would have others strictly corrected; but are not willing to be corrected ourselves.

The large liberty of others displeases us; and yet we would not be denied anything we ask for.

We are willing that others should be bound up by laws; and we suffer not ourselves by any means to be restrained.

Thus it is evident how seldom we weigh our neighbour in the same balance with ourselves.

If all were perfect, what then should we have to suffer from others for God's sake?

But now God has so disposed things, that we may learn to bear one another's burdens; for there is no man without defect; no man without his burden; no man sufficient for himself; no man wise enough for himself; but we must support one another, comfort one another, assist, instruct, and admonish one another.

But how great each one's virtue is, best appears by occasions of adversity: for occasions do not make a man frail, but show what he is.[22]

✠

The Lord asks of us only two things: love of His Majesty and love of our neighbor. These are what we must work for. By keeping them with perfection, we do His will and so will be united with Him. But how far, as I have said, are we from doing these two things! . . .

The most certain sign . . . as to whether or not we are observing these two laws is whether we observe well the love of neighbor. We cannot know whether or not we love God, although there are strong indications for recognizing that we do love Him; but we can know whether we love our neighbor. . . .

It's important for us to walk with careful attention to how we are proceeding in this matter, for if we practice love of neighbor

[22] Thomas à Kempis, *The Imitation of Christ*, ed. F. de Gonnelieu, S.J., trans. Fr. R. Challoner (Dublin: James Duffy, 1859), 1.16, 40–41.

with great perfection, we will have done everything. I believe that, since our nature is bad, we will not reach perfection in the love of neighbor if that love doesn't rise from love of God as its root.[23]

✠

Many souls, I am sure, will find here the reason for the difficulties, the bleakness, the slightness of the flowering of their interior life; they do not give themselves enough to Christ in the persons of His members; they hold themselves back too much. Let them give and it will be given to them, and given abundantly; for Christ Jesus does not let Himself be outdone in love. Let them rise above their selfishness, let them deliver themselves up to their neighbor with generosity, for God; and then Christ will deliver Himself up to them in plenitude. Because they forget self, Christ will take special care of them—and who better than He can lead us to beatitude?

It is no small thing to love our neighbour always and unfailingly; to do that needs a love that is strong and generous. Although love of God may in itself, because of the transcendence of its object, be more perfect than love of our neighbour, nevertheless, as the motive should be the same in the love which we bear for God and in that which we bear for our neighbor, often an act of love towards one's neighbor requires more intensity and gains more merit. Why is that? Because, God being beauty itself and goodness itself and He having shown us an infinite love, grace prompts us to love Him: whereas, in the case of our neighbour we are not without the possibility of encountering in him—or in us—obstacles resulting from different interests that surface between our neighbour and ourselves. These difficulties demand from the soul more fervour, more generosity, more forgetfulness of self and of the soul's own feelings and personal wishes; and that

[23] St. Teresa of Ávila, *The Interior Castle*, trans. Kieran Kavanaugh, O.C.D. and Otilio Rodriguez, O.C.D., The Classics of Western Spirituality (Mahwah, N.J.: Paulist Press, 1979), 3.8–9, 100.

is why love of neighbour, if it is to be maintained, requires more effort....

In a similar way, a super-natural love exercised toward one's neighbour despite repugnance, antipathy or natural differences of opinion shows, in the soul who possesses it, a greater intensity of Divine Life. I do not fear to say that a soul that delivers itself up supernaturally, unreservedly, to Christ in the person of its neighbour ... has a great love for Christ and is infinitely loved by Him. That soul will make great progress towards oneness with Our Lord. Whereas if you meet someone who devotes himself to frequent prayer and, despite that, voluntarily closes his heart to the necessities of his neighbour, you may take it for certain that a large degree of illusion is entering his prayer-life. For prayer has as its object simply the yielding up of the soul to the Divine Will. Now, in closing his heart to his neighbour, such a soul closes his heart to Christ, to the most sacred desire of Christ: "That they may be one ... that they may be made perfect in one." True holiness shines forth through charity and the entire gift of oneself.[24]

✠

I had never before fathomed the words of Our Lord: "The second commandment is like to the first: Thou shalt love thy neighbour as thyself." I had laboured above all to love God, and it was in loving Him that I discovered the hidden meaning of these other words: "Not every one that saith to me: Lord, Lord! shall enter into the Kingdom of Heaven, but he that doth the will of My Father." This will Our Lord revealed to me through the words of His new commandment addressed to His Apostles at the Last Supper, when He told them "to love one another as He had loved them." I set myself to find out how He had loved His Apostles, and I saw that it was not for their natural qualities, seeing they were but ignorant

[24] Bl. Columba Marmion, *Christ, the Life of the Soul*, trans. Alan Bancroft (Herefordshire: Gracewing, 2005), 457–458.

men, whose minds dwelt chiefly on earthly things. Yet He calls them His friends, His brethren; He desires to see them near Him in the Kingdom of His Father; and to open His Kingdom to them He wills to die on the Cross, saying: "Greater love than this no man hath, that a man lay down his life for his friends."

As I meditated on these divine words, I understood how imperfect was the love I bore my Sisters in religion, and that I did not love them as Our Lord does. Now I know that true charity consists in bearing all my neighbour's defects, in not being surprised at mistakes, but in being edified at the smallest virtues.

Above all else I have learnt that charity must not remain shut up in the heart, for "No man lighteth a candle and putteth it in a hidden place, nor under a bushel; but upon a candlestick, that they who come in may see the light." This candle, it seems to me, Mother, represents that charity which enlightens and gladdens, not only those who are dearest to us, but likewise all those who are of the household.

In the Old Law, when God told His people to love their neighbour as themselves, He had not yet come down upon earth; and knowing full well man's strong love of self, He could not ask anything greater. But when Our Lord gave His Apostles a new Commandment—"His own Commandment"—He not only required of us to love our neighbor as ourselves, but would have us love even as He does, and as He will do until the end of time.[25]

[25] St. Thérèse of Lisieux, *Saint Thérèse of Lisieux, the Little Flower of Jesus*, trans. Fr. Thomas N. Taylor (New York: P.J. Kenedy & Sons, 1926), 162–163.

15

Prayers

The Lord's Prayer

Our Father who art in Heaven, hallowed be Thy name. Thy Kingdom come. Thy will be done on earth as it is in Heaven. Give us this day our daily bread. And forgive us our trespasses, as we forgive those who trespass against us. And lead us not into temptation, but deliver us from evil. Amen.

Prayer to Obtain the Grace of a Devout Life

Grant me, O merciful God, to desire eagerly, to investigate prudently, to acknowledge sincerely, and to fulfill perfectly those things that are pleasing to Thee, to the praise and glory of Thy holy Name.

Do Thou, my God, order my life; and grant that I may know what Thou wilt have me to do; and give me to fulfill it as is fitting and profitable to my soul.

Grant me, O Lord my God, the grace not to falter either in prosperity or adversity; that I be not unduly lifted up by the one, nor unduly cast down by the other. Let me neither rejoice nor grieve at anything, save what either leads to Thee or leads away from Thee. Let me not desire to please anyone, nor fear to displease anyone save only Thee.

Let me never be deluded by the things that pass away, and let all things that are eternal be dear to me. Let me tire of that joy which is without Thee, neither permit me to desire anything that is outside Thee; and let all repose that is without Thee be tiresome to me.

Give me, my God, the grace to direct my heart toward Thee, and to grieve continually at my failures, together with a firm purpose of amendment.

O Lord my God, make me obedient without gainsaying, poor without despondency, chaste without stain, patient without murmuring, humble without pretense, cheerful without dissipation, serious without undue heaviness, active without instability, fearful of Thee without abjectness, truthful without double-dealing, devoted to good works without presumption, ready to correct my neighbor without arrogance, and to edify him by word and example without hypocrisy.

Give me, Lord God, a watchful heart which shall be distracted from Thee by no vain thoughts; give me a generous heart which shall not be drawn downward by any unworthy affection; give me an upright heart which shall not be led astray by any perverse intention; give me a stout heart which shall not be crushed by any hardship; give me a free heart which shall not be claimed as its own by any unregulated affection.

Bestow upon me, O Lord my God, an understanding that knows Thee, diligence in seeking Thee, wisdom in finding Thee, a way of life that is pleasing to Thee, perseverance that faithfully waits for Thee, and confidence that I shall embrace Thee at the last. Grant that my life be not without penances, that I may make good use of Thy gifts in this life by Thy Grace, and that I may partake of Thy joys in the glory of Heaven; Who livest and reignest God, world without end. Amen.[26]

[26] St. Thomas Aquinas, "Concede mihi, misericors Deus." See "*Concede mihi, misericors Deus*: For Ordering a Life Wisely," Michael Martin, https://www.preces-latinae.org/thesaurus/Varia/Concede.html.

Prayer for Enlightenment

Come, Holy Ghost, fill the hearts of Thy faithful: And enkindle in them the fire of Thy Love. Send forth Thy Spirit and they shall be created: And Thou shalt renew the face of the earth.

Let us Pray: O God, who hast taught the hearts of the faithful by the light of the Holy Ghost, give us by the same Spirit a love and relish of what is right and just, and the constant enjoyment of His comforts. Through Christ our Lord. Amen.

Prayer for Grace to Do the Will of God

Grant me, most kind Jesus, Thy grace, that it may abide with me, labor with me, and persevere with me to the end.

Grant me ever to desire and to will that which is the more acceptable to Thee, and pleases Thee more dearly.

May Thy will be mine, and my will ever follow Thine, and may I be unable to will or not will anything but what Thou willest or willest not.

Act of Charity

O My God, because Thou art the highest and most perfect good, I love Thee with my whole heart, and above all things; and rather than offend Thee, I am ready to lose all things; and moreover, for Thy Love I love, and will love, my neighbor as myself.

Christ's Prayer for His Disciples

I have given them thy word, and the world hath hated them, because they are not of the world; as I also am not of the world. I pray not that thou shouldst take them out of the world, but that thou shouldst keep them from evil. They are not of the world, as I also am not of the world. Sanctify them in truth.

Thy word is truth. As thou hast sent me into the world, I also have sent them into the world. And for them do I sanctify myself, that they also may be sanctified in truth. And not for them only do I pray, but for them also who through their word shall believe in me; That they all may be one, as thou, Father, in me, and I in thee; that they also may be one in us; that the world may believe that thou hast sent me. And the glory which thou hast given me, I have given to them; that they may be one, as we also are one: I in them, and thou in me; that they may be made perfect in one: and the world may know that thou hast sent me, and hast loved them, as thou hast also loved me. (John 17:14–23)

Prayer for Our Civil Authorities

We pray Thee, O God of might, wisdom, and justice, through whom authority is rightly administered, laws are enacted, and judgment decreed, assist, with Thy Holy Spirit of counsel and fortitude, the President of these United States, that his administration may be conducted in righteousness, and be eminently useful to Thy people over whom he presides, by encouraging due respect for virtue and religion; by a faithful execution of the laws in justice and mercy; and by restraining vice and immorality.

Let the light of Thy Divine Wisdom direct the deliberations of Congress, and shine forth in all the proceedings and laws framed for our rule and government; so that they may tend to the preservation of peace, the promotion of national happiness, the increase of industry, sobriety, and useful knowledge, and may perpetuate to us the blessings of equal liberty.

We recommend likewise to Thy unbounded mercy all our brethren and fellow-citizens, throughout the United States, that they may be blessed in the knowledge, and sanctified in the observance, of Thy most holy law; that they may be preserved in union, and in that peace which the world cannot give; and, after enjoying the blessings of this life, be admitted to those which are eternal.[27]

Prayer in Time of War

O Lord Jesus Christ, who in Thy Mercy hearest the prayers of sinners, pour forth, we beseech Thee, all grace and blessing upon our country and its citizens. We pray in particular for the President—for our Congress—for all our soldiers—for all who defend us in ships, whether on the seas or in the skies—for all who are suffering the hardships of war. We pray for all who are in peril or in danger. Bring us all after the troubles of this life into the haven of peace, and reunite us all together forever, O dear Lord, in Thy glorious Heavenly Kingdom.

Prayer for Peace

Give peace, O Lord, in our days; for there is none other that fighteth for us but only Thou, our God.

Let there be peace in Thy strength, O Lord.

And plenty in Thy strong places.

Let us Pray: O God, from whom proceed holy desires, right counsels, and just works; grant unto us, Thy servants, that peace which the world cannot give, that our hearts may be devoted to Thy service, and that, being delivered from the fear of our enemies, we may pass our time in peace under Thy protection. Through Christ our Lord. Amen.

[27] Archbishop John Carroll, "A Prayer for Our Government," 1791. See "Prayer for the Church and Civil Authorities," Priestly Fraternity of St. Peter, https://fssp.com/prayer-for-the-church-and-civil-authorities/.

The Greatest Commandment

Love One Another

As the Father hath loved me, I also have loved you. Abide in my love.

If you keep my commandments, you shall abide in my love; as I also have kept my Father's commandments, and do abide in his love.

These things I have spoken to you, that my joy may be in you, and your joy may be filled.

This is my commandment, that you love one another, as I have loved you.

Greater love than this no man hath, that a man lay down his life for his friends.

You are my friends, if you do the things that I command you.

I will not now call you servants, for the servant knoweth not what his lord doth. But I have called you friends: because all things whatsoever I have heard of my Father, I have made known to you.

You have not chosen me: but I have chosen you; and have appointed you, that you should go, and should bring forth fruit; and your fruit should remain: that whatsoever you shall ask of the Father in my name, he may give it you.

These things I command you, that you love one another. (John 15:9–17)

The Best of Fulton J. Sheen:
God Love You

✠

The mind must know,
but it never knows anything fully
until it knows God,
and the least knowledge of God
is worth more than
the knowledge of all created things.

—Fulton J. Sheen

16

The Basic Passion of All Is Love

Nothing worthwhile is ever accomplished without passion—and the basic passion of all is love.

Most people in the world are unloved. Some do not make themselves lovable because of their selfishness; others do not have enough Christian spirit to love those who do not love them. The result is that the world is full of lonely hearts. Here we speak not of love in the romantic or carnal sense, but in the higher sense of generosity, forgiveness, kindness, and sacrifice.

Once admit a purpose in life, and each and every act which tends toward that point bears the unmistakable stamp of joyfulness and cheer. The Christian has his fixed goal, namely, to make his life more and more Christ-like. His own nature is like a block of marble, and his will is the chisel. He looks out upon his model, Christ, and with the sharp points of his mortifying chisel, cuts away from his nature great huge chunks of cold selfishness, and then by finer and more delicate touches makes the great model appear forthwith, until finally only the brush of a hand is needed to give it its polished finish. There is no man living who has this Christian ideal who believes that repeated acts of faith, hope, and charity, prudence, justice, fortitude, and love are tainted with what the modern mind would call monotony. Each new conquest of self is a new thrill, for each repeated act brings closer and closer that love we fall just short of in all love, eternal union with Our Lord and Savior.

It is the winds and the winters which try the herbs, the flowers, and the trees, and only the strongest survive. So tribulation tries the soul, and in the strong, it develops patience, and patience, in its turn, hope, and hope finally begets love.

Love is to a great extent a stranger on earth; it finds momentary satisfactions in human hearts, but it soon becomes restless. It was born of the Infinite and can never be satisfied with anything less. In a certain sense, God spoiled us for any other love except Himself, because He made us out of His Divine Love.

Man never has loved, never will love anything he cannot get his arms around, and the cosmos is too big and too bulky. That is why the Immense God became a Babe in order that we might encircle Him in our arms.

One of the cruelest things that can happen to a human being is to be tolerated. Never once did Our Lord say, "Tolerate your enemies!" But He did say "Love your enemies: do good to them that hate you" (Matt. 5:44). Such love can be achieved only if we deliberately curb our fallen nature's animosities.

Christ said to man: "You give Me your humanity, I will give you My Divinity. You give Me your time, I will give you My Eternity. You give me your bonds, I will give you My Omnipotence. You give Me your slavery,

I will give you My Freedom. You give Me your death, I will give you My Life. You give Me your nothingness, I will give you My All." And the consoling thought throughout this whole transforming process is that it does not require much time to make us saints; it requires only much love.

✠

If we are to do good to others, they must be loved for God's sake. No moral profit comes from doing good to another because "he can get it for us wholesale" or from giving gifts to others because of the pleasure they give us. There is not even great merit in doing good to those who love us. "You love those who love you. Do not the heathens this?" (see Matt. 5:46–47). The greatest spiritual profit comes from loving those who hate us, and from giving gifts and dinners to those who cannot give anything in return, for then recompense will be made in the Kingdom of Heaven.

✠

Love is not to be measured by the joys and pleasures which it gives, but by the ability to draw joy out of sorrow, a resurrection out of a crucifixion, and life out of death. Unless there is a cross in our life, there will never be an empty tomb; unless there is the crown of thorns, there will never be the halo of light: "O, grave, where is thy victory? O, Death, where is thy sting?" (see 1 Cor. 15:55).

✠

If an egotist really understood the psychology of the human mind, he would never be heard to say that God is wrathful—for such a statement publishes his sinfulness. As a brown-colored glass can make the water in it seem brown, although it is not, so the Love that waits for us, passing through our sinful lives, may seem like wrath and anger. A change in our behavior removes all the unhealthy fear of God.

✠

Love that desires to limit its own exercise is not love. Love that is happier if it meets only one who needs help than if it met ten, and happiest if it met none at all, is not love. One of love's essential laws is expressed in the words of Our Lord that the Apostles fondly remembered after He ascended: "It is more blessed to give than to receive" (see Acts 20:35). Our nation will be happier and our hearts will be uplifted when we discover the true brotherhood of man, but to do this we must realize that we are a race of illegitimate children unless there is also the Fatherhood of God.

✠

The faithful loyal wife whose husband is snatched from her by death, the mother whose son refuses to visit her and bless her declining days with filial affection, the friend who has sacrificed all only to be betrayed by one for whom he gave all—all these experience the keenest and bitterest of all human sufferings: the pangs of unrequited love. Such victims can and really do die of a broken heart. But what is this love for another human being, compared to the love of God for man? The affection a human heart bears for another lessens as it multiplies the objects of its love, just as a river loses its fullness the more it divides itself into little streams. But with God, there is no decrease of love with the increase of objects loved, any more than a voice loses its strength because a thousand ears hear it.

✠

Saints love sinners, not because they both have vice in common, but because the saint loves the possible virtue of the sinner. The Son of God became the Son of Man because He loved man.

✠

If you are unhappy, or sad, or despondent, it is basically for only one reason: you have refused to respond to Love's plea: "Come to me, all you that labour, and are burdened, and I will refresh you. Take up my yoke upon you and learn of me, because I am meek, and humble of heart: and you shall find rest to your souls" (Matt. 11:28–29).

✠

By charity we do not mean kindness, philanthropy, generosity, or big-heartedness, but a supernatural gift of God by which we are enabled to love Him above all things for His own sake alone, and, in that love, to love all that He loves. To make it clear, we here set down the three principal characteristics of charity or supernatural love: (1) It is in the will, not in the emotions. (2) It is a habit, not a spasmodic art. (3) It is a love relationship, not a contract.

Because charity is in the will, you can command it, which you cannot do with natural likes or dislikes. A little boy cannot help disliking spinach, as perhaps you cannot help disliking sauerkraut, and as I cannot help disliking chicken. The same is true of your reactions to certain people. You cannot help feeling an emotional reaction against the egotistical, the sophisticated, and the loud, or those who run for first seats or snore in their sleep.

✠

Show love to others, and everyone seems lovable. The law of physics that every action has a contrary and equal reaction has its psychological counterpart. If we sow the seed of distrust in society, society always returns the harvest of distrust. The emotional reprises of others can be used as the mirror of our own interior dispositions.

✠

Every love rests on a tripod. Every love has three bases or supports: goodness, knowledge, and similarity.

✠

Do we really understand the nature of love? Have we not sometimes, in great moments of affection for a little child, said in language which might vary from this, but which expressed the idea, "I love that child so much, I should just like to possess it within myself?" Why? Because all love craves for unity. In the natural order, God has given great pleasures to the unity of the flesh. But those are nothing compared to the pleasure of the unity of the spirit, when divinity passes out to humanity, and humanity to divinity—when our will goes to Him, and He comes to us, so that we cease to be men and begin to be children of God.

If there has ever been a moment in your life when a fine, noble affection made you feel as if you had been lifted into the third or the seventh Heaven; if there has ever been a time in your life when a noble love of a fine human heart cast you into an ecstasy; if there has ever been a time when you have really loved a human heart—then I ask you, think of what it must be to be united with the great Heart of Love! If the human heart in all of its fine, noble, Christian riches can so thrill, can so exalt, can make us so ecstatic, then what must be the great Heart of Christ? Oh, if the spark is so bright, what must be the flame!

✠

To love what is below the human, is degradation; to love what is human for the sake of the human, is mediocrity; to love the human for the sake of the Divine, is enriching; to love the Divine for its own sake is sanctity.

✠

The greatest joys of life are purchased at the cost of some sacrifice. No one ever enjoys good reading, good music, or good art without a certain amount of study and effort. Neither can one enjoy love without a certain amount of self-denial. It is not that love by its nature demands suffering, for there is no suffering in Divine Love. But whenever love is imperfect, or whenever a body is associated with a soul, there must be suffering, for such is the cost of love's purification. One cannot grow from ignorance to love of poetry without discipline. Neither can one mount from one level of love to another without a certain amount of purification. The Blessed Virgin passed from one level of love which was for her Divine Son, to the higher level of a love for all whom He would redeem, by willing His Passion and death at the Marriage Feast of Cana.

✠

How life changes its meaning when we see the love of the flesh as the reflection of the Eternal Light shot through the prism of time! They who would separate the earthly sound from the Heavenly harp can have no music; they who believe that love is only the body's breath soon find love breathes its last and they have made a covenant with death. But they who see in all earthly beauty the faint copy of divine loveliness; they who see in fidelity to every vow, even when the other is untrue, a proof that God loves us who are so unlovable; they who, in the face of their trials, see that God's love ended in a cross; they who allow the river of their rapture to broaden out the blended channels of prayer and worship—these will, even on earth, learn that Love was made flesh and dwelled amongst us. Thus, Love becomes an ascension toward that blessed day when the limitless depths of our souls will be filled with the boundless giving, in one eternal now, where love is life's eternity and God is Love.

✠

False isolation of the part from its whole is a common trait in contemporary thought. Man's life nowadays is divided into many compartments which remain ununited and unintegrated. A businessman's business has no connection with his life in the family—so little in fact that his wife (his "little wife") is kept ignorant of her husband's income. As there is no connection between a man's profession and the rest of his daily existence, neither is there a connection between his daily life and religion. This chopping up of life into watertight compartments becomes more disastrous as occupation and work are related, less and less, to a strictly human ideal; mechanization plays a catastrophic role. There is a double love in each of us—a love that is self-realizing and looks to our own good, and a love that is self-effacing and looks to the good of another. Both loves are included in the Divine Command, "Thou shalt love thy neighbor as thyself" (Matt. 22:39). The one love is self-assertive and possessive—it makes us eat, drink, and work to sustain our life. The other love is sacrificial or possessed and seeks not to own but to be owned, not to have but to be had. The first takes water that it may live. The other shares or even gives up the water that the neighbor may live.

✠

The most degraded man on the face of the earth is precious, and Christ died for Him. That poor soul may have made the wrong choice, but that is not for us to decide. While he has life, he has hope. He might not seem lovable to us, but he is loved by God.

✠

Self-preservation is one of the first laws of nature, and it implies a legitimate self-love; for if we did not love ourselves, we could not continue to live. Our Divine Lord reminded us to love our neighbors as we love ourselves. Self-love, knowing it cannot exist by itself any more than the stomach can exist without food, extends itself in one direction by the acquiring of knowledge; and the more we know of the truth, the more our personality is developed. The quest for perfection of the self reaches to the infinite. No one has ever said, "I know enough." That is why we hate to have secrets kept from us (men hate this just as much as women). We are incurably curious; we were made to know.

✠

What does it mean to be a Christian? Christianity is not a system of ethics; it is a life. It is not good advice; it is divine adoption. Being a Christian does not consist in being kind to the poor, going to Church, reading the Bible, singing hymns, being generous to relief agencies, just to employees, gentle to cripples, serving on Church committees, though it includes all of these. It is first and foremost a *love relationship*.

As you can never become a member of a family by doing generous deeds, but only by being born into it out of love, so you can never become a Christian by doing good things, but only by being born to it through Divine Love.

✠

When you fail to measure up to your Christian privilege, be not discouraged for discouragement is a form of pride. The reason you are sad is because you looked to yourself and not to God; to your failing, not to His Love. You will shake off your faults more readily when you love God than when you criticize yourselves. The sick person looks happily at the physician, not at his wounds. You have always the right to love Him in your heart, even though now and then you do not love Him in your acts. Keep no accounts with God or you will always be so hopelessly in debt as to be bankrupt.

17

Pleasure Comes from Without, but Joy Comes from Within

Pleasure comes from without, but joy comes from within, and it is, therefore, within the reach of everyone in the world.

One of the greatest mistakes is to think that contentment comes from something outside us rather than from a quality of the soul. There was once a boy who only wanted a marble; when he had a marble, he only wanted a ball; when he had a ball, he only wanted a top; when he had a top, he only wanted a kite; and when he had the marble, the ball, the top, and the kite, he still was not happy.

Trying to make a discontented person happy is like trying to fill a sieve with water. However much you pour into it, it runs out too rapidly for you to catch up.

Two considerations are helpful in developing a good disposition. The first is to be mindful that a happy conscience makes a happy outlook on life, and an unhappy conscience makes us miserable on the inside and everyone else miserable on the outside. When our conscience bothers us, whether we admit it or not, we often try to justify it by correcting others, or by finding fault with them. The readiness to believe evil about others is in large part ammunition for a thousand scandals in our own hearts. But by finding black spots in others, they believe they distract attention from their own miserable state. The good conscience, on the contrary, finds good in others even when there is some discontent with self.

Joy can be felt in both prosperity and adversity. In prosperity, it consists not in goods we enjoy but in those we hope for; not in the pleasures we experience but in the promise of those which we believe without our seeing. Riches may abound, but those for which we hope are the kind which moths do not eat, rust consume, nor thieves break through and steal (see Matt. 6:19–20). Even in adversity, there can be joy in the assurance that the Divine Master Himself died through the Cross as the condition of His Resurrection.

The secret of peace of soul is to combine detachment from evil with attachment to God, to abandon egotism as the ruling, determining element in living, and to substitute Our Divine Lord as the regent of our actions. What is anti-God must be repressed; what is Godly must be expressed. Then one will no longer awaken with a dark brown taste in the mouth or a feeling of being run-down at the heels. Instead of greeting each day with the complaint, "Good God, morning!" he will say, from the happiness of a soul in love, "Good morning, God!"

The condition of having a good time is that one shall not be always trying to have a good time.

✠

Contentment comes in part from faith—that is, from knowing the purpose of life and being assured that whatever the trials are, they come from the hand of a Loving Father. Secondly, in order to have contentment, one must also have a good conscience. If the inner self is unhappy because of moral failures and unatoned guilt, then nothing external can give rest to the spirit. A third and final need is mortification of desires, the limitation of delights. What we over-love, we often over-grieve. Contentment enhances our enjoyment and diminishes our misery. All evils become lighter if we endure them patiently, but the greatest benefits can be poisoned by discontent. The miseries of life are sufficiently deep and extensive without our adding to them unnecessarily.

✠

The pursuit of pleasure is a token of man's higher nature, a symptom of his loneliness in this world. Torn between what he has, which surfeits him, and the far-off Transcendent, which attracts him, every worldly man stands in grave danger of self-hatred and despair until he finds his true infinite in God. As Pascal put it: "The knowledge of God without that of our misery produces pride. The knowledge of our misery without that of God gives despair. The knowledge of Jesus Christ is intermediate, because therein we find God and our misery."[28]

✠

It is not so much what happens in life that matters; it is rather how we react to it. You can always tell the character of a person by the size of the things that make him mad. Because modern man lives in a world which has reference to nothing but itself, it follows that when depression, war, and death enter into his two-dimensional world, he tumbles into the most

[28] Blaise Pascal, *Thoughts*, in *Works of Pascal: The Thoughts, Letters, and Opuscules of Blaise Pascal*, trans. O. W. Wright (New York: Hurd and Houghton, 1869), 334.

hopeless despair. A man can work joyfully at a picture puzzle, so long as he believes the puzzle can be put together into a composite whole. But if the puzzle is a hoax, or if it was not made by a rational mind, then one would go mad trying to work it out. It is this absence of purpose in life which has produced the fear and frustration of the modern mind.

✠

Everyone must have pleasure, the philosophers tell us. The man who has integrated his personality in accordance with its nature, and oriented his life toward God knows the intense and indestructible pleasure the saints called joy. No outward event can threaten him or ruffle his happiness. But many men look outward for their pleasure and expect the accidents of their lives to provide their happiness. Since nobody can make the universe his slave, everyone who looks outward for pleasure is bound to disappointment. A glut of entertainment wearies us; a realized ambition becomes a bore; a love that promised full contentment loses its glamor and its thrill. Lasting happiness can never come from the world. Joy is not derived from the things we get or the people we meet; it is manufactured by the soul itself, as it goes about its self-forgetful business.

✠

Pleasures must be arranged in a hierarchy if we are to get the greatest enjoyment out of life. The most intense and lasting joys come only to those who are willing to practice a certain self-restraint, to undergo the boredom of a preliminary discipline. The best view is from the mountain top, but it may be arduous to reach it. No man ever enjoyed reading Horace without drilling himself with the declensions of his grammar first. Full happiness is understood only by those who have denied themselves some legitimate pleasure in order to obtain deferred joys. Men who "let themselves go," go to seed or go mad. The Savior of the world Himself told us that the best joys come only after we have purchased them by prayer and fasting: we must give up our copper pennies first, out of love for Him, and He will pay us back in pieces of gold, in joy and ecstasy.

✠

It is hard to understand why God should seemingly care so much for sinners; but does not a mother rejoice more at the recovery of her sick child than at the continued health of the rest of the family? Did not the Prodigal Son get the fatted calf, while the one who stayed at home was not so much as given a goat?

18

The Mind Must Know, but It Never Knows Anything Fully Until It Knows God

The mind must know, but it never knows anything fully until it knows God, and the least knowledge of God is worth more than the knowledge of all created things. If we knew what the sun was, we would not need to know what its ray is; if we knew the ocean, we would know the chemistry of a drop of water; if we knew the circle, we would know what the smallest arc is; and in knowing God, we know all things.

Knowledge is in the mind; character is in the will. To pour knowledge into the mind of a child, without disciplining his will to goodness, is like putting a rifle into the hands of a child. Without education of the mind, a child could be a stupid devil. With education of the mind, but without love of goodness, a child could grow up to be a clever devil.

This whole problem of the dignity of man was thought out years ago by Aristotle, who called man a microcosm or a little universe, because he contained the cosmos within himself. Man sums up the lower order of creation in a double way: first, physically, and secondly, mentally. Physically, he is made up of a combination of chemicals, vegetative processes, and animal activities; he is like matter, because he exists; like plants, because he lives; and like animals, because he feels. But he is above all these because he has his own peculiar perfection; namely, an intelligence, which enables him to know not only the phenomena of earth and the movements of the Heavens, but the intelligibility of these phenomena in terms of causes and, in particular, in terms of the First Cause, God.

✠

It is a law of nature that no one ever gets his second wind until he has used up his first wind. So it is with knowledge. Only when we practice the moral truths which we already know will a deeper understanding of those truths and a fuller revelation come to us. Each new height the mind reveals must be captured by the will before greater heights come into view. Religion, then, is not just a subject of discussion; it is a subject for decision. There is a progress here, as in all research. Our knowledge of Truth will be cumulative, if we really wish it to grow. "Ask, and it shall be given you; seek, and you shall find: knock, and it shall be opened to you" (Matt. 7:7).

✠

Man is distinguished from the animals by the possession of a rational soul which gives him his special human dignity. It is fitting that the principal effects of the infusion of Divine energy should be manifested in the two main faculties of the soul—the intellect and the will. Once the Divine Power penetrates the intellect, it becomes Faith; once it infuses the will, it becomes Hope and Charity. Thus are born the three great supernatural virtues, by which we can believe in God, and know Him, and love Him.

✠

There is only one reason for being critical, and that is to be constructive, just as the only reason for razing a house is to make one rise in its place.

Character grows by leaps and bounds as soon as one has ferreted out the master egotisms and removed the disguises of the superficial self. Self-knowledge is really the reversal of criticism from those around us to ourselves. Observing the neighbor's faults raises our ego; as we depress the ego and face our own predominant fault, the neighbor who before seemed hateful takes on a new lovableness. By losing our own pride and vanity, we gain a world of friends.

The mind can know things beyond experience.

Excesses affect the reason in four ways: by perverting the understanding so that one becomes intellectually blind and unable to see the truth; by weakening prudence and a sense of values, thus producing rashness; by building up self-love to generate thoughtlessness; by weakening the will until the power of decision is lost and one becomes a prey to inconstancy of character.

Tradition is not, as some believe, a heritage of the Dark Ages, something that cabins and confines thought; rather, it is a memory. A sense and an intellectual memory are indispensable conditions of all right thinking. We are under the necessity of going back to the storehouse of our mind for past impressions and thoughts in order to build up the present thought. What is true of the individual is true of society. Tradition is the memory of society, and without that tradition, society cannot think. "It is owing to tradition," says Pascal, "that the whole procession of men in the course of so many centuries may be considered as a single man who always subsists and who learns continually."[29]

[29] Blaise Pascal, *Pensées et Opuscules*, ed. Léon Brunschvicg (Paris: Hachette, 1912), 80.

The will, which is the seat of inclination, in belief, is never blind according to traditional philosophy. The intellect supplies its object and the reason of its belief, for nothing is willed unless it is known. It will be recalled that, for St. Thomas, the will is nobler than the intellect in those cases where the object of the will is nobler than the soul. The reason is, that the intellect drags things down to its level, but the will always goes up to meet the requirements of its love. Thus it is nobler to love God than to know all created things, for in loving God the will goes out to meet God, but in knowing things it descends to the finite and the material.

Are the schools and universities throughout countries that ignore God really educating the young men and women entrusted to their care? Would we say that a man was a learned mathematician if he did not know the first principles of Euclid? Would we say that a man was a profound physicist if he did not know the first principles of light, sound, and heat? Can we say that a man is truly educated who is ignorant of the first principles of life and truth and love—which is God?

19

There Is Only One Thing Definitely and Absolutely Your Own, and That Is Your Will

There is only one thing in the world that is definitely and absolutely your own, and that is your will. Health, power, possessions, and honor can all be snatched from you, but your will is irrevocably your own, even in Hell. Hence, nothing really matters in life, except what you do with your will.

No character or temperament is fixed. To say "I am what I am, and that I must always be," is to ignore freedom, Divine Action in the soul, and the reversibility of our lives to make them the opposite of what they are.

We are never tempted beyond our strength. Every moral failure is ours alone, because our choices are our own.

In the very nature of things, ethics and morality can exist only upon the condition of a veto. Bravery, for example, is possible only in a world in which a man may be a coward. Virtue is possible only in a world where a man may be vicious. Sacrifice is possible only in that order in which a man may be selfish. Love is possible only when it is possible not to love.

Cold statues cannot love. It is the possibility of saying No which gives so much charm to the heart when it says Yes. A victory may be celebrated only on those fields in which a battle may be lost. Hence, in the divine order of things, God made a world in which man and woman would rise to moral heights, not by that blind driving power which makes the sun rise each morning, but rather by the exercise of that freedom in which one may fight the good fight and enjoy the spoils of victory, for no one shall be crowned unless he has struggled.

An acorn works out its destiny naturally: it grows to be an oak. Man, however, is free to stunt his growth, and to choose another end than the efflorescence of his faculties in union with Perfect Love. If man chooses, he need not grow up to be an oak; he can remain a poor sapling or just a "poor sap."

The human heart is torn between a sense of emptiness and a need of being filled, like the waterpots of Cana. The emptiness comes from the fact that we are human. The power of filling belongs only to Him who ordered the waterpots filled. Lest any heart should fail in being filled, Mary's last valedictory is: "Whatsoever He shall say to you, do ye" (John 2:5). The heart has a need of emptying and a need of being filled. The power of emptying is human—emptying in the love of others—the power of filling belongs only to God. Hence all perfect love must end on the note: "Not my will, but Thine be done, O Lord!" (see Luke 22:42).

Self-discipline may be defined as a struggle against evil inclinations in order to subject them to our own will and ultimately to the will of God.

The modern world is opposed to self-discipline on the ground that personality must be "self-expressive." Self-expression is right so long as it does not end in self-destruction. A boiler that would be self-expressive by blowing up, or an engine that would be self-expressive by jumping the tracks, would both be acting contrary to their natures as fashioned by the minds of the engineers who designed them. So, too, if man acts contrary to what is best and highest in his nature by rebelling against the Eternal Reason of God, his Creator, his self-expression is self-destruction.

✠

In self-discipline *you "give up" nothing*. You merely "exchange." You find that you can get along without an excess of drink, but you cannot give up peace of mind or union with God, so you "exchange" one for another. "What exchange shall a man give for his soul?" (Matt. 16:26).

✠

Bad temper is an indication of a man's character; every man can be judged by the things which make him mad. Heaven could be ruined by one single soul who was *touchy*.

✠

Self-discipline is really self-expression—expression of all that is highest and best in self; the farmer plows under the weeds for the completest expression of the corn's desire to grow. Self-control, through mortification or asceticism, is not the rejection of our instincts, passions, and emotions, nor is it thrusting these God-given impulses into unconsciousness. Our passions, instincts, and emotions are good, not evil; self-control means only curbing their inordinate excesses.

✠

The difference between people who never get the breaks and those who make every now an occasion for thanking God is this: the latter live in an area of love greater than their desire to "have their way." As a waif on the streets suffers misfortunes which the child in a loving family does not know, so the man who has not learned to place full trust in God suffers reverses and disasters which would not appear as troubles to loving souls. God does not show Himself equally to all creatures. He does show all men how to turn everything to joy. This does not mean God is unfair, but only that it is impossible for even Him to show Himself to certain hearts under some conditions. The sunlight has no favorites, but it cannot shine as well on a dusty mirror as on a polished one. In the order of Divinity, there is nothing accidental; there is never a collision of blind forces, hurting us, at random. There is, instead, the meeting of a Divine Will and a human will which has a perfect trust that ultimate good is meant for it, although it may not understand how until eternity.

Many people today have taken as their goal the obtainment of wealth. This is an inferior "destination," for it reduces man's dignity, making him serve something lesser than himself—for material goods are inferior to human personality. Other people chase after honors, publicity, and fame. These are also unsatisfying and unworthy goals; anyone who steps into a shower, where he cannot carry his press clippings, knows that his celebrity has not elevated him above other men. To make "what people say" an aim in life is to court a nervous breakdown by becoming the slave of every copywriter's whim.

The beauty of this universe is that practically all gifts are conditioned by freedom. The one word in the English language which proves the close connection between gifts and freedom is: "Thanks." As Chesterton said: "If man were not free," he could never say, "Thank you for the mustard."[30]

Self-discipline does not mean self-contempt or destruction of personality, but it rather aims at self-expression in the highest sense of the term.

[30] See G.K. Chesterton, "The Maniac," chap. 2 in *Orthodoxy* (Chicago: Moody, 2009).

Christian character is nothing more nor less than the reconciling of opposite virtues. In other words, a really great character is not just a brave man, for if a man were brave without being tender, he might very easily become cruel. Tenderness is what might be called the other wing to bravery. In like manner, majesty alone does not make character, for majesty without gentleness might very soon degenerate into pride. Love of Peace alone does not make character, for without the opposite virtue of courage, peacefulness could very easily slip into a spineless cowardice. Wisdom without simplicity makes a man proud; simplicity without wisdom makes a man a simpleton. A real character, therefore, does not possess a virtue on a given point on the circumference without, at the same time possessing the complementary virtue which is diametrically opposed to it; for what is character, but the tension between opposites, the equilibrium between extremes.

Freedom has lost its value for the modern world. It understands freedom too often as the right to do whatever you please, or the absence of constraint. This is not freedom but license, and very often anarchy. Freedom means not the right to do what you *please*, but the right to do what we *should* in order to attain the highest and noblest ends of our nature.

Every moment comes to you pregnant with a Divine purpose; time being so precious that God deals it out only second by second. Once it leaves your hands and your power to do with it as you please, it plunges into eternity, to remain forever whatever you made it.

God's knowledge that you shall act in a particular manner is not the immediate cause of your acting, any more than your knowledge that you are sitting down caused you to sit down, or prevents you from getting up, if you willed to do it.

✠

Circumstances must not control you; you must control circumstances. *Do* something to them! Even the irritations of life can be made stepping stones to salvation. An oyster develops a pearl because a grain of sand irritated it. Cease talking about your pains and aches. Thank God for them! An act of thanksgiving when things go against our will, then a thousand acts of thanksgiving when things go according to our will.

✠

You will never be happy if your happiness depends on getting solely what you want. Change the focus. Get a new center. Will what God wills, and your joy no man shall take from you. "So also you now indeed have sorrow; but I will see you again, and your heart shall rejoice; and your joy no man shall take from you. And in that day you shall not ask me anything. Amen, amen I say to you: if you ask the Father any thing in my name, he will give it to you. Hitherto you have not asked any thing in my name. Ask, and you shall receive; that your joy may be full" (John 16:22–24).

✠

We are all on the roadway of life in this world, but we travel in different vehicles: some in trucks, some in jeeps, some in ambulances; others in twelve-cylinder cars, and others in flivvers. But each of us does the driving.

✠

It is typically American to feel that we are not doing anything unless we are doing something big. But from the Christian point of view, there is no one thing that is bigger than any other thing. The bigness comes from the way our wills utilize things.

✠

The modern man is so confused that, for all his talk about freedom, he is often eager to renounce this gift in favor of security. Even when no greater security is offered him in exchange, he is eager to give up his freedom of choice; he cannot bear the burden of its responsibility. Weary of being alone and afraid and isolated in a hostile world, he wants to surrender himself to something or to somebody—to commit a kind of mayhem of the will. Will he surrender to the anonymous authority of a collective State, or will he accept a spiritual authority which restores his freedom with the acceptance of truth?

✠

Life may be likened to children playing. The totalitarian would build them a playground where all their movements are supervised, where they are ordered to play only those games which the State dictates—games which the children nearly all detest. The result is that freedom of choice is, of course, lacking; but in addition, all hope and spontaneity are lost to the children.

✠

For those who wish to cultivate the virtue of temperance and to be self-possessed, these two specific recommendations are made: First, each day practice at least three trivial mortifications, for example, giving up the ninth cigarette, holding back the sarcastic word, returning a kindly answer to a sneer, or sealing the lips on the scandal you just heard, which probably, like all scandals, is 99.5 percent untrue.

Second, the magnitude of the mortification is not as important as the love of God for which it is done. Great sacrifices without love are worthless for the soul; nor because they are great does it follow they were done with love; it is the motive that matters—do them out of love of God.

✠

Temperance must not be confused with Puritanism, which because of the abuse of a thing would take away its use; nor with license, which would interpret all restraint as an infringement of liberty. Rather, there is a golden mean, as revealed in Our Lord's first miracle at Cana where He changed water into wine to satisfy the individual appetite and blessed the married couple for the satisfaction of the creative instinct.

The higher our loves and ideals, the nobler will be our character. The problem of character training is fundamentally the inculcation of proper ideals. That is why every nation holds up its national heroes, that citizens may become like to them in their patriotism and devotion to country.

If we have heroes and ideal prototypes for those who love sports, the stage, country, army, and navy, why should there not be an ideal in the all-important business of leading a good life and saving our souls?

Now what are you *really*? You are what you are, not by your emotions, your feelings, your likes and dislikes, but by your *choices*. The decisions of your free will will be the content of your judgment.

The *virtue* of Hope is quite different from the *emotion* of Hope. The emotion centers in the body and is a kind of dreamy desire that we can be saved without much effort. The virtue of Hope, however, is centered in the *will* and may be defined as a divinely infused disposition of the will by which with sure confidence, thanks to the powerful help of Almighty God, we expect to pursue eternal happiness, using all the means necessary for attaining it.

20

Human Love Is a Spark from the Great Flame of Eternity

Life is not a snare nor an illusion. It would be that only if there were no Infinite to satisfy our yearnings. Everyone wants a love that will never die and one that has no moments of hate or satiety. That love lies beyond humans.

Human love is a spark from the great flame of Eternity. The happiness which comes from the unity of two in one flesh is a prelude to that greater communion of two in one spirit. In this way, marriage becomes a tuning fork to the song of the angels, or a river that runs to the sea. Then it is evident that there is an answer to the elusive mystery of love and that somewhere there is a reconciliation of the quest and the goal, and that is in final union with God, where the chase and the capture, the romance and the marriage, fuse into one. For since God is boundless, Eternal Love, it will take an ecstatic eternal chase to sound its depths.

✠

Peace is a fruit of love, and love flowers in the man oriented toward God. The greatest privilege that can come to man is to have his life God-directed; this follows when he has remotely paved the way by disciplined self-direction. God cares enough for us to regulate our lives—and this is the strongest proof of love that He could give us. For it is a fact of human experience that we do not care very much about the details of other people's lives unless we love them. We are not deeply interested in hearing more of those individuals whom we meet in the subway and in the street and on the highway. But as soon as we begin to know and love any of them, then we become more and more interested in their lives; we have a greater care for them. As we bring them into the area of our love, both our interest and their happiness increases. It is like this when we bring ourselves into the area of God's love: there is an increasing Divine guidance of the details of our life, and we are ever being made more sure of the depth and reality of His Love.

There are few things more beautiful in life than to see that deep passion of man for woman which begot children as the mutual incarnation of their love, transfigured into that deeper "passionless passion and wild tranquility" which is God.

The basic error of mankind has been to assume that only two are needed for love: you and me, or society and me, or humanity and me. Really it takes three: self, other selves, and God; you, and me, and God.

Love that is only giving, ends in exhaustion; love that is only seeking, perishes in its selfishness.

If we start with the belief that most people in the world are crooks, it is amazing how many crooks we find. If, however, we go into the world with the assumption that everyone is nice, we are constantly running into nice people. To a great extent, the world is what we make it. We get back what we give. If we sow hate, we reap hate; if we scatter love and gentleness, we harvest love and happiness. Other people are like a mirror which reflects back on us the kind of image we cast. The kind man bears with the infirmities of others, he never magnifies trifles and avoids a spirit of fault-finding. He knows that the trouble with most people in the world is that they are unloved. No one cares for them either because they are ugly or nasty, or troublesome, or so-called bores. To a great extent, their character is made by the resentment they feel to others who are unkind. One of life's greatest joys comes from loving those whom no one else loves. Thus do we imitate Our Heavenly Father Who certainly cannot see much in any of us creatures that is very attractive.

✠

Love never grows old, except to those who put its essence into that which grows old: the body. Like a precious liquid, love shares the lot of the container. If love is put in a vessel of clay, it is quickly absorbed and dried; if, like knowledge, it is placed in the mind, it grows through the years, becoming stronger, even as the body grows weaker. The more it is united with the spirit, the more immortal it becomes.

✠

Man is much more inclined to concentrate his moral actions in one great moment and thereby often wins the merit of a hero. The woman, on the contrary, scatters her tiny little sacrifices through life and multiplies them to such an extent that very few give her the credit for sacrifice because it has been so multiplied.

✠

True love always imposes restrictions on itself—for the sake of others—whether it be the saint who detaches himself from the world in order more readily to adhere to Christ, or the husband who detaches himself from former acquaintances to belong more readily to the spouse of his choice. True love, by its nature, is uncompromising; it is the freeing of self from selfishness and egotism. Real love uses freedom to attach itself unchangeably to another. St. Augustine has said: "Love God, and then do whatever you please." By this, he meant that, if you love God, you will never do anything to wound him. In married love, likewise, there is perfect freedom and yet one limitation which preserves that love, and that is the refusal to hurt the beloved.

✠

God, Who made the sun, also made the moon. The moon does not take away from the brilliance of the sun. The moon would be only a burnt-out cinder floating in the immensity of space, were it not for the sun. All its light is reflected from the sun. The Blessed Mother reflects her Divine Son; without Him, she is nothing. With Him, she is the Mother of Men. On dark nights we are grateful for the moon; when we see it shining, we know there must be a sun. So in this dark night of the world when men turn their backs on Him Who is the Light of the World, we look to Mary to guide their feet while we await the sunrise.

✠

If you ever want to know the real qualities of a man, judge him not by his attitude to the world of commerce, his outlook on business, his kindness, and his gentle manners, but judge him rather by his attitude to his own mother.

✠

What mysterious power is it that a mother has over a son that, when he confesses to guilt, she strives to minimize it, even when it shocks her heart at the perversity of the revelation? The impure are rarely tolerant of the pure, but only the pure can understand the impure.

✠

The problem of a woman is whether certain God-given qualities, which are specifically hers, are given adequate and full expression. These qualities are principally devotion, sacrifice, and love. They need not necessarily be expressed in a family, nor even in a convent. They can find an outlet in the social world, in the care of the sick, the poor, the ignorant—in the seven corporal works of mercy.

✠

The unalterable fact is that no woman is happy unless she has someone for whom she can sacrifice herself—not in a servile way, but in the way of love. Added to the devotedness is her love for creativeness. A man is afraid of dying, but a woman is afraid of not living. Life to a man is personal; life to a woman is otherness. She thinks less in terms of perpetuation of self and more in terms of perpetuation of others—so much so, that in her devotedness she is willing to sacrifice herself for others. To the extent that a career gives her no opportunity for either, she becomes defeminized. If these qualities cannot be given an outlet in a home and a family, they must nevertheless find other substitutions in works of charity, in the defense of virtuous living, and in the defense of right, as other Claudias enlighten their political husbands. Then woman's work as a money earner becomes a mere prelude and a condition for the display of equity, which is her greatest glory.

✠

We love to see ourselves idealized in the minds of others. That is one of the beautiful joys of love. We become fresh, innocent, brave, strong in the mind of the beloved. Love covers up the corruption of the soul. The winter of discontent is forgotten by being clothed in the blossoms of a new spring. After a while, the lover begins to substitute what really is in his own mind, with what he is in the mind of the other. It is this idealization which pleases in love. That is why love gives an incentive to betterment. When the other thinks well of us, we try to be worthy of that opinion. The fact that others assume us to be good is a great incentive to goodness. That is why, too, one of the basic principles of life ought to be to assume goodness in others; thus we make them good.

✠

Sex is one of the means God has instituted for the enrichment of personality. It is a basic principle of philosophy that there is nothing in the mind which was not previously in the senses. All our knowledge comes from the body. We have a body, St. Thomas tells us, because of the weakness of our intellect. Just as the enrichment of the mind comes from the body and its senses, so the enrichment of love comes through the body and its sex. As one can see a universe mirrored in a tear on a cheek, so in sex can be seen mirrored that wider world of love.

✠

Fidelity in marriage implies much more than abstention from adultery. All religious ideals are positive, not negative. Husband and wife are pledges of eternal love. Their union in the flesh has a grace which prepares and qualifies both souls for the union with God. Salvation is nothing but wedlock with God. All those who have taken hold of Christ in marriage wear a "yoke that is sweet and a burden that is light" (see Matt. 11:30). As yokemates of love, they pull together in the tilling of the field of the flesh, until there is finally revealed to them the full splendor of harvest in eternal union with God.

✠

Marriage must end in the family, at least in intention if not in act; for only through the family does life escape exhaustion and weariness by discovering its duality to be trinity, by seeing its love continually reborn and reknown, by having its mutual self-giving transformed into receiving. Love thus defeats death, as it defeats exhaustion. It achieves a kind of immortality as self-renewal becomes self-preservation. God is eternal society; Three Persons in one Divine Nature. The family is human society; mutual self-giving which ends in self-perfection.

✠

The equation of man with the animal is a great fallacy; sex in man is not the same as sex in animals. An animal feels, but no animal loves. In the animal, there is no body-mind conflict; in man, there is. In the animal, sex is mechanical, a matter of stimulus and response. In man, it is linked with mystery and freedom. In the animal, it is only a release of tension; in man, its occurrence is determined by no natural rhythm, but by the will. Sex can cause a loneliness and sadness in man which it cannot cause in an animal.

21

Faith Will Answer the Principal Problems of Your Life: Why? Whence? Whither?

Faith will answer the principal problems of your life: Why? Whence? Whither? If you are without faith, you are like a man who lost his memory and is locked in a dark room waiting for memory to come back. There are a hundred things you can do: scribble on the wallpaper, cut your initials on the floor, and point to the ceiling. But if you are ever to find out why you are there, and where you are going, you will have to enlarge your world beyond space and time. There is a door out of that room. Your reason can find it. But your reason cannot create the light that floods the room, nor the new world in which you move, which is full of signs on the roadway to the City of Peace and Eternal Beatitude with God.

Have you noticed that as men lose faith in God, they become selfish, immoral, and cruel? On a cosmic scale, as religion decreases, tyranny increases; as men lose faith in Divinity, they lose faith in humanity. Where God is outlawed, there man is subjugated.

You have exactly the same eyes at night as you have in the day, but you cannot see at night, because you lack the additional light of the sun.

So, too, let two minds with identically the same education, the same mental capacities, and the same judgment, look on a Host enthroned on an altar. The one sees bread, the other sees Christ, not, of course, with the eyes of the flesh, but with the eyes of faith. Let them both look on death: one sees the end of a biological entity, the other an immortal creature being judged by God on how it used its freedom. The reason for the difference is: one has a light which the other lacks, namely, the light of faith.

The things that happen to us are not always susceptible to our minds' comprehension or wills' conquering; but they are always within the capacity of our faith to accept and of our wills' submission.

The evil which God permits must not be judged by its immediate effects, but rather by its ultimate effects. When you go to a theater, you do not walk out because you see a good man suffering in the first act. You give the dramatist credit for a plot. Why cannot you do that much with God?

Philosophy gives a proof for the existence of God; the science of apologetics gives the motives for believing in Christ, the Son of God; but all the incontrovertible proofs they offer fall short of the certitude that actually comes to a convert through the gift of Faith.

The cruelest master is the man who never learned to obey, and the severest judge is the man who never examines his own conscience. The man who is conscious of his need of absolution is the one who is most likely to be indulgent to others.

✠

The world is full of those who suffer unjustly and who through no fault of their own bear the "slings and arrows of outrageous fortune."[31] What should be our attitude to those who speak untruly of us, who malign our good names, who steal our reputations, and who sneer at our acts of kindness?

The answer is to be found in the first word from the Cross: *forgive*. If there was ever anyone who had a right to protest against injustice, it was He Who is Divine Justice; if ever there was anyone who was entitled to reproach those who dug His hands and feet with steel, it was Our Lord on the Cross.

✠

The only times some people think of God are when they are in trouble, or when their pocketbook is empty, or they have a chance to make it a little fatter. They flatter themselves that at such moments they have faith when really they have only earthly hope for good luck. It cannot be repeated too often: faith bears on the soul and its salvation in God, not on the baubles of earth.

✠

The real test of the Christian is not how much he loves his friends, but how much he loves his enemies.

✠

Christ so loved us that He took our sins upon Himself as if He were guilty, and draws us freely to repentance by the price He paid to save us. Hence forgiveness is no glib thing! The Cross was the supreme expression of the righteousness of God!

[31] William Shakespeare, *Hamlet*, act 3, scene 1.

If the redemption of man were done without cost, it would insult us, for no man with a sense of justice wants to be "let off." It would insult God, for the whole moral order founded on justice would be impugned. The Cross is the eternal proof that no sin is forgiven through indifference.

✠

If the sense of guilt is an estrangement from God and sorrow at having wounded someone we love, if the ache of self-reproach is a symptom of our rejection of love's invitation, then our emphasis must be not so much on the guilt, as on the way to remove it and find peace. It takes love to see that love has been hurt. Divine Love always rewards that recognition by forgiveness; and once the forgiveness is given, a relationship is restored in a much more intimate way than ever before.

✠

Our Lord deals separately with each soul. The crown of gold we want may have underneath it the crown of thorns, but the heroes who choose the crown of thorns often find that underneath it is the crown of gold.

✠

If we knew ourselves better, we would be more forgiving of others. The harder we are on ourselves, the easier we will be on others; the man who has never learned to obey knows not how to command; and the man who has never disciplined himself knows not how to be merciful.

✠

You may sin a thousand times and be forgiven, but like the man who threw himself into a river a hundred times, each time to be rescued by the bridge-tender, you may be told by the rescuer: "Someday you will throw yourself into the river and I may not be here to pull you out."

✠

Even those that seem to be without a cross actually have one.

✠

Our Lord never tried to induce the poor to accept poverty as a good, or misery as a thing to be sought for itself. He glorified neither the poor man nor the rich man. But the one He did praise was the poor man who, having once been rich, had willingly made himself poor—the poor man who, by detaching himself from everything, became possessed of everything—the man who, wanting nothing, owned all things. For Our Lord does not canonize the "giving up" of wealth in favor of a vacuum; He approves, rather, of giving wealth in exchange for the far greater riches of Heaven. He did not tell us "Blessed are the poor," or "Blessed are the rich." But He told us, "Blessed are the poor in spirit" (Matt. 5:3).

✠

We think too often that in Heaven there is going to be somewhat the same equality in social positions that we have here; that servants on earth will be servants in Heaven; that the important people on earth will be the important people in Heaven.

✠

Regardless however of how multiplied or grievous your sins may have been, there is still room for hope. Did not Our Lord say: "For I came not to call the just, but sinners" (Mark 2:17); and on another occasion, "There shall be joy in heaven upon one sinner that doth penance, more than upon ninety-nine just who need not penance (Luke 15:7). If He forgave the thief, and Magdalene, and Peter, why not you? What makes many in old age sad is not that their joys are gone, but that their hopes are gone.

✠

God loves us too much to leave us comfortable in our sins. Because the violinist wants the best from his violin, he tightens its strings in penitential disciplines, until they can give forth the perfect note; if endowed with consciousness, the violin would probably protest the sacrifice it had to make in preparation for the perfection it was destined to attain. We are like the violin.

Here is a psychological suggestion for acquiring peace of soul. Never brag; never talk about yourself; never rush to first seats at table or in a theatre; never use people for your own advantage; never lord it over others as if you were better than they. These are but popular ways of expressing the virtue of humility, which does not consist so much in humbling ourselves before others as it does in recognizing our own littleness in comparison to what we ought to be.

A disappointment, a contradiction, a harsh word, an undeserved rebuke, a pain, a loss borne patiently in His name and endured as in His presence is worth more than any prayer said by the lips.

One of the last acts of Our Lord was to wash the feet of His Disciples, after which he told them that out of such humiliation true greatness is born.

In silence, there is humility of spirit or what might be called a "wise passiveness." In such the ear is more important than the tongue.

Our happiest times are those in which we forget ourselves, usually in being kind to someone else. That tiny moment of self-abdication is an act of true humility: the man who loses himself finds himself and finds his happiness.

The Lord hears us more readily than we suspect; it is our listening to Him that needs to be improved. When people complain that their prayers are not heard by God, what often has happened is that they did not wait to hear His answer.

✠

We can hammer iron, because it is material; we can melt ice, because we can warm it with our fires; we can break twigs, because we can get them into our hands, but we cannot crucify Faith, we cannot melt Hope, we cannot murder Justice, because all these things are spiritual and therefore beyond the power of enslavement.

In a higher sense, the soul of every man is the last and impregnable fortress of character. As long as he wills to keep his spirit his own, no one can take it away, even though they take his life.

✠

Why does God not always answer our prayers for an increase in salary, for larger commissions, for more money? Why did He not answer the prayer of the thief on the left to be taken down from the cross, and why did He answer the prayer of the thief on the right to forgive his sins?

Because material favors draw us away from Him, but the cross always draws us to Him.

✠

We do not pray in order that we may change God's Will; we pray rather to change our own.

✠

When God does answer your prayers of petition, do you ever thank Him for His gift?

✠

Prayer is that which establishes contact with Divine Power and opens the invisible resources of Heaven.

✠

A higher form of prayer than petition — and a potent remedy against the externalization of life — is meditation. Meditation is a little like a daydream or a reverie, but with two important differences: in meditation, we do not think about the world or ourselves, but about God. And instead of using the imagination to build idle castles in Spain, we use the will to make resolutions that will draw us nearer to one of the Father's mansions. Meditation is a more advanced spiritual act than "saying prayers."

✠

We begin to act differently when we recognize the immensity of our possibilities. Our whole life changes then, like that of a farmer when he discovers oil on what he had previously believed to be just a poor farm. Prayer overcomes sadness by putting us in relation with the Eternal, and then the change occurs. Before, we had thought ourselves unloved by anyone; now, we know that we are loved by God.

✠

Our pride makes us look down on people, so that we can never look up to God. In fact because our pride admits no law and no authority other than ourselves, it is essentially anti-God.

All our other sins can be from ourselves; for example, avarice, lust, anger, gluttony. But pride comes direct from Hell. By that sin fell the angels. It destroys the very possibility of conversion. If therefore we can humble ourselves as did the thief at the right, and admit we have done wrong, then out of our creative despair we can cry to the Lord to remember us in our misery! The very moment we stop strutting and posing and begin to see ourselves as we really are, then in our humility, we shall be exalted.

22

Nothing Ever Happens to the World Which Did Not First Happen Inside the Mind of Some Man

As society is made by man, so man, in his turn, is made by thoughts, his decisions, and his choices. Nothing ever happens to the world which did not first happen inside the mind of some man: the material of the skyscraper merely completes the architect's dream. Even the material of our physical selves is the servant of our thoughts: psychologists recognize the fact that our bodies may become tired only because of tiredness in the mind. Worry, anxiety, fear, and boredom are felt as physical: mind fatigue appears to us as bodily fatigue.

✠

Our happiness consists in fulfilling the purpose of our being. Every man knows, from his own unfulfilled hunger for them, that he was built with a capacity for three things of which he never has enough. He wants life—not for the next few minutes, but for always, and with no aging or disease to threaten it. He also wants to grasp truth—not with a forced choice between the truths of mathematics or geography, but he wants all truth. Thirdly, he wants love—not with a time limit, not mixed with satiety or disillusionment, but love that will be an abiding ecstasy.

✠

Man is the highest creature on earth: he matters more than every theory; every government, every plan for the world, and all that it contains are not worth one immortal soul. Let institutions crumble, blueprints go up in smoke, and governments decay. These are mere trivia, compared to the vast question asked of all of us: "How is a man the better for it, if he gains the whole world at the cost of losing his own soul?" (see Mark 8:36).

✠

Man has his feet in the mud of the earth, his wings in the skies. He has sensations like the beasts and ideas like the angels, without being either pure beast or pure spirit. He is a mysterious composite of body and soul, with his body belonging to a soul, and his soul incomplete without the body.

✠

Man is animated by an urge, an unquenchable desire to enlarge his vision and to know the ultimate meaning of things. If he were only an animal, he would never use symbols, for what are these but attempts to transcend the visible? No, he is a "metaphysical animal," a being ever longing for answers to the last question. The natural tendency of the intellect toward truth and of the will toward love would alone signify that there is in man a natural desire for God. There is not a single striving or pursuit or yearning of the human heart, even in the midst of the most sensual pleasures, that is not a dim grasping after the Infinite. As the stomach yearns for food and the eye for light and the ear for harmony, so the soul craves God.

✠

Men live by their desires, but it is possible for us to choose whether we will desire things of the spirit or of the world. The man or woman who can look back on his day and count five times when he has refused to yield to some minute whim is on the way to inner growth: he has held himself back and rejected the slavery of things.

✠

Only those people who believe in transcendent reality can pass through this life with a sure sense of humor. The atheist, the agnostic, the skeptic, the materialist—all these have to take themselves seriously; they have no spiritual vantage point on which they can stand, look down upon themselves, and see how laughable they are. There is nothing more ludicrous than pretentiousness, and unless self-knowledge comes to puncture it, the absurdity will grow. Yet, if our self-exaltation is deflated without a recognition of the Mercy of God, Who can lift up the sinner, then it may beget despair: God is required for cheerfulness.

✠

The use to which we put what we have is closely related to what we are, to our "being," and to what we will become. He who keeps everything he has for himself must lose it all at death; he who has given it away will get it back in the coin of immortality and joy.

✠

Man is the only creature in the visible universe who can know himself—can turn around and observe his own thoughts, as it were, in a mirror. A stone, a tree, an animal—such things cannot turn back in their thoughts to identify themselves, nor can they contemplate themselves or stand off and regard themselves as an object. But the human spirit can penetrate itself; it can be not only a subject but also the object of a thought; it can admire itself, be angry with itself, and even despair of itself. This capacity for self-reflection, which animals do not have, makes man superior to the animal but also makes him subject to mental disorders when the soul does not fulfill the high destiny to which it is called—when it refuses to use the human faculty of unprejudiced examination of the self and its acts. To surrender this activity is to move down from the human level to that of the animal; to replace the I with the ego; to enter into the realm of mental eccentricity.

✠

There is no surer formula for discontent than to try to satisfy our cravings for the ocean of infinite Love from the teacup of finite satisfactions. Nothing material, physical, or carnal can ever satisfy man completely; he has an immortal soul which needs an eternal Love. "Not in bread alone doth man live" (Deut. 8:3; Matt. 4:4). Man's need for Divine Love, once perverted, impels him to go on seeking infinite Love in finite beings—never finding it, yet not able to end the search despite his disappointments. Then follow cynicism, boredom, ennui, and finally despair. Having lost spiritual oxygen, such a man suffocates. Life ceases to mean anything precious to him, and he thinks of doing away with himself as his last and final act of rebellion against the Lord of Life.

✠

The truth of the matter is not that God is hard to find, but rather that man is afraid of being found. That is why we so very often hear in Sacred Scripture the words "Fear not." At the very beginning of Divine Life in Bethlehem, the angels found it necessary to warn the shepherds, "Fear not." In the midst of Our Lord's public life, He had to tell His frightened Apostles, "Fear not." And after His Resurrection, He had to preface His words on peace with the same injunction, "Fear not."

Our Lord finds it necessary to warn us not to fear because there are three false fears that keep us away from God: (1) We want to be saved, but not from our sins. (2) We want to be saved, but not at too great a cost. (3) We want to be saved in our way, not His.

✠

If our lives just "end," our friends will ask: "How much did he leave?" But if our life is "finished" our friends will ask: "How much did he take with him?" A finished life is not measured by years but by deeds; not by the time spent in the vineyard, but by the work done. In a short time, a man may fulfill many years; even those who come at the eleventh hour may finish their lives; even those who come to God like the thief, at the last breath, may finish their lives in the Kingdom of God. Not for them the sad word of regret: "Too late, O ancient Beauty, have I loved Thee."[32]

✠

Pride is of two kinds: it is either the pride of omniscience or the pride of nescience. The pride of omniscience tries to convince your neighbor you know everything; the new pride of nescience tries to convince your neighbor that he knows nothing. The latter is the technique used by "sophomores" who pride themselves on the fact that man can know nothing. Hence, they doubt everything, and of this, they are very sure. They seem to forget that the doubting of everything is impossible, for doubt is a shadow, and there can be no shadow without light.

✠

By the Divine standard, true greatness is indicated neither by the possession of great abilities nor the buzz of popular applause. Any talent a person has, such as a talent for singing, speaking, or writing, is a gift of God. He has done nothing more to merit it than a child with a beautiful face. "If then, thou hast received, why dost thou glory, as if thou hadst not received it?" (1 Cor. 4:7). The richer the gifts, the greater the responsibilities on the Day of Judgment.

✠

Men crave wealth—they have a hundred times more than they need, and still, they want more, and their wanting it makes them unhappy. Even the loss of the least of it robs them of joy, as the plucking of a single hair from a head that is full of it, gives pain. Nothing ever comes up to our expectations.

Well, why is it? The reason is that in looking forward to the things of this world, we use our imagination, which, as a faculty of the soul, is spiritual, and therefore capable of imagining infinite things.

[32] St. Augustine of Hippo, *Confessions*, 10.27.

There comes to every human, at one period or another, the discovery of his nothingness. The man who wanted a certain position eventually becomes dissatisfied with it and wants something higher; he who has wealth does not have enough, not even with the first million. So in married love, there comes the crisis of nothingness which comes to everyone, whether he is married or not, and does not mean that life is to be mocked. *One has not hit the bottom of life, but only the bottom of one's ego.* One has not hit the bottom of his soul, but only of his instinct; not the bottom of his mind, but of his passions; not the bottom of his spirit, but of his sex. The aforementioned trials are merely so many contacts with reality which Almighty God sends into every life, for what we are describing here is common to every life. If life went on as a dream without the shock of disillusionment, who would ever attain his final goal with God and perfect happiness? The majority of men would rest in mediocrity; acorns would be content to be saplings; some children would never grow up and nothing would mature.

There is nothing so dangerous for a civilization as softness, and there is nothing so destructive of personality as a want of discipline. Arnold Toynbee, the historian, tells us that out of twenty-one civilizations which have vanished, sixteen collapsed because of decay within. Nations are not often murdered; they more often commit suicide. That is the sinister meaning of our present mood of selfishness and love of pleasure, our affirmation of our own egotism, our widespread refusal to discipline the self. Although two world wars have imposed upon us many sacrifices which we have accepted willingly, even these have not been sufficient to make us perform the greatest sacrifice of all—to give up the illusion that a man is most self-expressive when he allows the animal to gain mastery over the spirit.

Fortitude may be defined as that virtue which enables us to face undismayed and fearlessly the difficulties and dangers which stand in the way of duty and goodness. It stands midway between foolhardiness, which rushes into danger heedlessly, and cowardice, which flees from it recreantly. Because fortitude is related to bravery, it must not be thought that bravery is devoid of fear; rather it is control of fear. Fortitude is of two kinds, depending upon whether it is directed to a natural good or a supernatural good.

A soldier, for example, who braves the dangers of battle for love of country practices natural fortitude. But the saint who overcomes all difficulties and dangers for the sake of the glory of God and the salvation of his soul practices supernatural fortitude.

23

There Can Be No World Peace Unless There Is Soul Peace

Unless souls are saved, nothing is saved; there can be no world peace unless there is soul peace. World wars are only projections of the conflicts waged inside the souls of modern men, for nothing happens in the external world that has not first happened within a soul.

God will not allow unrighteousness to become eternal. Revolution, disintegration, chaos must be reminders that our thinking has been wrong, our dreams have been unholy. Moral truth is vindicated by the ruin that follows when it has been repudiated. The chaos of our times is the strongest negative argument that could ever be advanced for Christianity. Catastrophe becomes a testimony to God's power in a meaningless world, for by it God brings a meaningless existence to naught. The disintegration following an abandonment of God thus becomes a triumph of meaning, a reaffirmation of purpose. Adversity is the expression of God's condemnation of evil, the registering of Divine Judgment. As Hell is not sin, but the effect of sin, so these disordered times are not sin, but the wages of sin. Catastrophe reveals that evil is self-defeating; we cannot turn from God without hurting ourselves.

✠

Jews, Protestants, and Catholics alike, and all men of goodwill, are realizing that the world is serving their souls with an awful summons—the summons to heroic efforts at spiritualization. An alliance among Jews, Protestants, and Catholics is not necessary to fight against an *external* enemy, for our "wrestling is not against flesh and blood; but against principalities and powers, against the rulers of the world of this darkness, against the spirits of wickedness in the high places" (Eph. 6:12).

We desire unity of religion but not when purchased at the cost of the unity of the truth. But we plead for a unity of religious peoples, wherein each marches separately according to the light of his conscience, but strikes together for the moral betterment of the world; a unity through prayer, not hate. If Satan has his fellow travelers, then why should not God and His Divine Son? The Roman sergeant who built a temple for the Jews was a fellow traveler with them in their belief in God. The woman at Tyre and Sidon became a fellow traveler of Christ. The forces of evil are united; the forces of good are divided. We may not be able to meet in the same pew—would to God we could—but we can meet on our *knees*.

✠

The communion of men one with another is a consummation devoutly to be wished, but it can never be achieved on a compulsory basis, or by the exterior organization of society, which impoverishes human personality and negates the spiritual in man. The rebirth of a new order cannot start with the denial of man, but with his reaffirmation as made to the Divine Image. No better start can be made than with the Christian doctrine that a man is more precious than the universe, that the universe exists for him, that society can use some human functions, but never at the cost of absorption, and that even in his evil moments man is worth addressing in the second person singular, as Our Lord did the thief in that beautiful affirmation of democracy on the Cross: "This day *thou* shalt be with Me in Paradise" (Luke 23:43; emphasis mine).

✠

Communism should not be met by vituperation, name-calling, and personal hate. Hate is like a seed—it grows. By hating Communists we advance Communism, for Communism grows in discord just as disease thrives in dirt. As Manzoni wrote: "There are few things that corrupt a people so much as a habit of hatred."[33] Only a spurious distinction between individual and social morality has made possible the appeal to hate in the struggle of nations.

Pius XII, in his Christmas Message of 1940, declared that one of the first victories to be won is "victory over hate which is today dividing the nations."[34] Communism is an ideology and as such is intrinsically wicked, but Communists are persons, made to the image and likeness of God and, therefore, should be subjects of our kindness and charity, that we may prove ourselves worthy children of the Heavenly Father. There is no erring soul that cannot attain to the treasures of Redemption. It is precisely out of love for the sinner that the sin is hated. "The very fact that we hate in our brother his fault and the absence of good is because of our love of our brother."[35] Not even the violence of Communism abrogates, but rather renders more imperative, the Christian law.

✠

Freedom had its roots in man's spiritual nature, before there was ever a liberal, a democrat, a Fascist, a Communist, or a Nazi. Freedom does not arise out of any social organization or any constitution or any party, but out of the soul of man.

✠

A nation always gets the kind of politicians it deserves. When our moral standards are different, our legislation will be different. As long as the

[33] Alexander Manzoni, *A Vindication of Catholic Morality* (London: Keating and Brown, 1836), 79.

[34] Pius XII, Allocution to the College of Cardinals (December 24, 1940).

[35] St. Thomas Aquinas, *Summa Theologica* II-II, q. 34, art. 3.

decent people refuse to believe that morality must manifest itself in every sphere of human activity, including the political, they will not meet the challenge of Marxism.

America's greatest enemy is not from without, but from within, and that enemy is hate: hatred of races, peoples, classes, and religions. If America ever dies, it will be not through conquest but suicide.

To the extent that psychoanalysis, in the twentieth century, takes an interest in the inside of a man's soul, it represents a great progress over the sociologies of the nineteenth century, which thought that everything that was wrong in the world was due to poverty, bad economic conditions, free trade, high tariffs, or politics. Furthermore, to the extent that psychoanalysis has revealed the effects of our minds—even of the unconscious mind—on our physical health and behavior, it has confirmed the great Christian truth that an uncontrolled mind (or even an uncontrolled unconsciousness) leads to abnormality.

Many psychiatrists today know very well that all they have to do to help certain distressed minds is to listen to their stories. Convince the anxious heart that you know the secret of his anxiety and he is already half cured. Convince the enemy that we have no bitterness in our heart against him and his arm will fall helpless at his side. All mental abnormalities have their roots in selfishness, all happiness has its roots in kindness. But to be really kind, one must see in everyone an immortal soul to be loved for God's sake. Then everyone is precious.

The sense of justice is so deep-rooted in us that if we are not good, we try to pacify our consciences by attributing the same evil to others. Charity, on the contrary, is unsuspicious; and, because it believes in others, is most encouraging of good. Charity never imputes the evil motive, never judges solely by externals.

✠

No one has a right to talk on the subject of persecution unless he condemns it wherever he finds it, and irrespective of who is persecuted, whether it be a Jew, a Protestant, or a Catholic. Persecution is not essentially anti-Semitic, it is not essentially anti-Christian. It is anti-human.

✠

Our Divine Lord was interested in studying the almsgivers and it was the quality of their giving which arrested Him, far more than the quantity they gave. He had once said that where our treasure is, there our heart is, also. Now He tells us that where the heart goes, there the treasure follows. Few of us have His attitude toward alms; we do not trouble to read the list of donors in fine type under the heading, "*Amounts less than* . . ." But probably that would be to Him the most important section of the list; on that occasion in the Temple He immortalized a gift of two of the smallest coins in the ancient world.

✠

True greatness is measured not by superiority but by service: "And he that will be first among you, shall be your servant" (Matt. 20:27). The greatest race on earth is the race that renders the most service to others in the name of God.

✠

Our Lord never discoursed on equality: He spoke to the Samaritans, ate with publicans and sinners, and offered His life for *all* men.

✠

Do not think of God as always looking around corners with an angel as a secretary to jot down all your sins. He is also looking at your good deeds, seeing every drink of cold water you give in His name, every visit to the sick you make in His name, every act of kindness you do for your fellowman in His name.

✠

By a peculiar paradox, as the home loses its authority, the authority of the State becomes tyrannical. Some moderns would swell their ego into infinity; but at Nazareth Infinity stoops down to earth to shrink into the obedience of a child.

✠

Our relations with external things are all in terms of having or of not having; the inner life of the spirit centers, in contrast, on being, on what one is. Too often people spoil their whole lives in desires to have, when our main interests should be devoted to efforts to be. Since nothing in the material universe is greater than the spirit, the personality within each of us, every yielding of ourselves to some material craving or necessity is a loss. Having anything at all creates problems; the more keys a man carries on his key ring, the more numerous his problems. And not having things we think we need can cause frustration, too. But the man who wants nothing is free; whatever happens to him is acceptable, and whatever is withheld from him is surrendered without a pang.

✠

There are only two things that could possibly remove evil and suffering from the world: either the conformity of human wills to the will of God, or God becoming a dictator and destroying all human wills.

Why is it that men, who, by forgetting the Love of God, turn the universe into a house of mass suicide, never think of blaming themselves, but immediately put God on the judgment seat, and question His Love and Goodness?

We all have a share in the evils of the world, and it ill behooves us to ignore our faults and become critics of God. It is we who are in the prisoners' dock in a world crisis like this. Instead of questioning the God of Love, we ought to be throwing ourselves on the Mercy of His Judgment.

✠

Traditionally, all gossips are women; but men are often guilty of the same offense. They call it "judging."

✠

Nothing that is given in a spirit of generosity is ever lost.

✠

Every task we undertake has two aspects—our purpose, which makes us think it worth doing, and the work itself, regarded apart from its end-purpose. We play tennis to get exercise; but we play the game as well as possible, just for the joy of doing the thing well. The man who argued that he could get as much exercise by sloppy technique on the courts would have missed an understanding of the second aspect of all activity: the accomplishment of the task in accordance with its own standards of excellence. In the same way, a man working in an automobile factory may have, as his primary purpose, the earning of wages; but the purpose of the work itself is the excellent completion of the task. A workman should be aware of the second purpose at all times—as the artist is aware of the aim of beauty in his painting and the housewife is aware of the need for neatness when she dusts.

✠

Repose—true leisure—cannot be enjoyed without some recognition of the spiritual world. For the first purpose of repose is the contemplation of the good—its goal is a true perspective, the small incidents of everyday life in their relation to the larger goodness that surrounds us. Genesis tells us that after the creation of the world, "God saw all the things that he had made, and they were very good" (Gen. 1:31). Such contemplation of his work is natural to man, whenever he, too, is engaged in a creative task. The painter stands back from his canvas, to see whether the details of the seascape are properly placed. True repose is such a standing back to survey the activities that fill our days.

Some souls try to escape the reproaches of conscience by an excessive activity, even to the point of jitters and neurotic overwork. Happy people work, sometimes very hard, in the fulfillment of their duties. But others use work as a drug to keep their thoughts off their own conscience, their inner misery. When work is done for its own delight or to provide the economic necessities, it is normal; but when it is a compulsive escape from inner guilt, it ceases to be work and becomes an addiction. Normal work takes a man outside of himself, exteriorizes his ego, unites him with reality, and atones for his sins. But abnormal activity is one of the means a fearful ego uses in the effort to lose itself.

Work should, in justice, receive two kinds of reward—for it is not only individual, but also social. John Jones, who works in a mine, is tired at the end of the day: this is his individual sacrifice. For it, he receives his wages. But John Jones has also, during the day, made a social contribution to the economic well-being of the country and the world. For this social contribution, John Jones today is given nothing ... although he has a moral right to a share of the social wealth his work creates. We need a modification of the wage system, so that the worker may share in the profits, ownership, or management of his industry. When labor leaders and capitalists thus agree together to give labor some capital to defend there will no longer be two rival groups in industry; labor and management will become two cooperating members working together, as the two legs of man cooperate to help him walk.

Matter divides, as spirit unites. Divide an apple into four parts, and it is always possible to quarrel as to who has the biggest part; but if four men learn a prayer, no one man deprives the other of possessing it—the prayer becomes the basis of their unity. When the goal of civilization consists not in union with the Heavenly Father, but in the acquisition of material things, there is an increase in the potentialities of envy, greed, and war. Divided men then seek a dictator to bring them together, not in the unity of love, but in the false unity of the three Ps—Power, Police, and Politics.

✠

To work truly for the good of society, one must be carried away by enthusiasm for something outside society. Humanism of itself is insufficient. Detachment from the individual can be accomplished by attachment to society, but detachment from society can be accomplished only by attachment to God. For this reason, there never was enunciated a principle better destined to affect social disinterestedness than that of Him Who said: "Seek ye therefore first the Kingdom of God, and His justice, and all these things shall be added unto you" (Matt. 6:33).

24

God Never Refuses Grace to Those Who Honestly Ask for It

God never refuses grace to those who honestly ask for it. All He asks is that the vague thirst for the Infinite which has urged the soul on to seek its good in a succession of pleasures shall now be transformed into a thirst for God Himself. All we need do is to voice these two petitions: Dear Lord, illumine my intellect to see the Truth, and give me the strength to follow it. It is a prayer that is always answered. And it makes no difference whether the desire for God we voice has come from our disgusts, satieties, and despair or whether it is born of our love of the beautiful, the perfect. God is willing to take either our old bones or our young dreams, for He loves us, not because of the way we are, but because of what we can be through His Grace.

✠

It is a strange paradox, but a true one, nevertheless, that man only becomes most human when he becomes most divine, because he has been destined from all eternity to be conformable to the image of the Son of God. Any form of Humanism, therefore, which denies the necessity of grace, and attempts to perfect man without it, is asking man to grow without an environment in which to grow. To remain on the level of the purely human, and to hold up the ideal of "decorum," is to permit man to expand horizontally, in the direction of the human, but not vertically, in the direction of the Divine. Humanism allows for the spreading out of man on the plane of nature, but not for his being lifted up on the plane of grace, and elevation is far more important than expansion. Deny the order of grace, the realm of the Fatherhood of God, and what environment has humanity to grow in except poor weak humanity like himself? Since the soul is spiritual, man needs the environment not only of humanity, which belongs to the realm of his body, but that of spirit, which belongs to his soul, and it is only by entering into harmony with that great environment that he attains the end of his creation.

✠

God walks into your soul with silent step. God comes to you, more than you go to Him. Every time a channel is made for Him, He pours into it His fresh gift of grace. And it is all done so undramatically—in prayer, in the Sacraments, before the altar, in loving service of fellow man.

Never will His coming be what you expect, and yet never will it disappoint. The more you respond to His gentle pressure, the greater will be your freedom.

✠

As long as the soul dominates the body, as long as man follows the dictates of right reason, man lives a moral existence naturally. But experience bears out what Revelation teaches, namely that man cannot keep the whole moral law over a long period of time without falling into sin. Man therefore needs help from above and aids which nature cannot supply, and this higher life which gives strength to the soul is grace. It makes us children of God, partakers of the Divine Nature, and heirs of Heaven. Grace is the life of Christ in the soul. We said before that man lives naturally when the life of the soul dominates the life of the body: here we add that man lives supernaturally as long as the life of Christ dominates the soul and through it all nature. It is thanks to this participated life of God in the soul through grace that even the human body takes on a new dignity.

✠

The reason why we are not better than we are is that we do not will to be better: the sinner and the saint are set apart only by a series of tiny decisions within our hearts. Opposites are never so close as in the realm of the spirit: an abyss divides the poor from the rich, and one may cross it only with the help of external circumstances and good fortune.

The dividing line between ignorance and learning is also deep and wide: both leisure to study and a gifted mind would be required to turn an ignoramus into a learned man. But the passage from sin to virtue, from mediocrity to sanctity, requires no "luck," no help from outer circumstances. It can be achieved by an efficacious act of our own wills in cooperation with God's grace.

✠

As all men are touched by God's flaming love, so all are also touched by the desire for His intimacy. No one escapes this longing; we are all kings in exile, miserable without the Infinite. Those who reject the grace of God have a desire to avoid God, as those who accept it have a desire for God.

✠

The major problem of the world is the restoration of the *image of man*. Every time a child is born into the world, there is a restoration of the human image, but only from the physical point of view. The surcease from the tragedy can come only from the restoration of the spiritual image of man, as a creature made to the image and likeness of God and destined one day, through the human will in cooperation with God's grace, to become a child of God and an heir of the Kingdom of Heaven.

✠

The secret of growing old is this counsel an old man once gave a youth: "Repent on your last day." But the youth answered: "But who knows when is my last day?" For that reason said the Saint: "Repent today for it would be tomorrow."

✠

Many persons identify themselves with their environment. Because life is good to them, they believe they are good. They never dwell on eternity because time is so pleasant. When suffering strikes, they become divorced from their pleasant surroundings and are left naked in their own souls. They then see that they were not really affable and genial, but irritable and impatient. When the sun of outer prosperity sank, they had no inner light to guide their darkened souls. It is, therefore, not what happens to us that matters; it is how we react to it.

No one is better because of pain; conceivably a man may become seared and scarred by pain. But, the very emptiness of soul that follows enforced divorce from pleasurable surroundings does drive the soul back unto itself, and if it cooperates with grace at that moment, it may find the meaning of life.

✠

One day a woman went to the saintly Fr. John Vianney, the Curé of Ars, in France, and said: "My husband has not been to the Sacraments or to Mass for years. He has been unfaithful, wicked, and unjust. He has just fallen from a bridge and was drowned—a double death of body and soul." The Curé answered: "Madam, there is a short distance between the bridge and the water, and it is that distance which forbids you to judge."

✠

Will eternity be anything like what I have seen, or what I have heard, or what I can imagine? No, eternity will be nothing like anything I have seen, heard, or imagined. Listen to the voice of God: "That eye hath not seen, nor ear heard, neither hath it entered into the heart of man, what things God hath prepared for them that love him" (1 Cor. 2:9).

✠

Revolution within the soul is the Christian adventure. It requires no hatred, demands no personal rights, claims no exalted titles, tells no lies.

In such a revolution, it is love which bores from within and acts as a Fifth Column, loyal to God, within our tangled and disordered selves. Such a revolution destroys the pride and selfishness, the envy and jealousy, and longing to be "first" which makes us intolerant of others' rights. The sword it carries is not turned against our neighbor, but against our absurd overvaluation of the self. In other revolutions, it is easy to fight, for it is against the "evil enemy" that we are at war. But the Christian revolution is difficult, for the enemy we must assault is a part of us. Yet this is the only revolution that ever issues in true peace; other rebellions are never ended, for they stop short of their goal: they leave hatred still simmering in the soul of man.

It is so easy to lose Christ; He can even be lost by a little heedlessness; a little want of watchfulness and the Divine Presence slips away. But sometimes a reconciliation is sweeter than an unbroken friendship. There are two ways of knowing how good God is: one is never to lose Him, the other is to lose Him and find him again.

God solicits each of us by a dialogue no other soul can hear. His action on the soul is always for us alone. He sends no circular letters, uses no party lines. God never deals with crowds as crowds—they could give Him only earthly glory—but what He wants is each soul's singular and secret fealty. He calls His sheep by name; He leaves the ninety-nine that are safe to find the one that is lost. On the Cross, He addresses the thief in the second person singular: "This day thou shalt be with Me in Paradise" (Luke 23:43).

Every person has a destiny—a final destiny. He has lesser goals, too, such as making a living, rearing a family, but over and above all, there is his supreme goal, which is to be perfectly happy. This he can be if he has a life without end or pain or death, a truth without error or doubt, and an eternal ecstasy of love without satiety of loss. Now this Eternal Life, Universal Truth, and Heavenly Love is the definition of God. To refuse this final project and to substitute a passing, incomplete, unsatisfying object, such as flesh or ambitious ego, is to create an inner unhappiness that no psychiatrist can heal.

An animal seeks pleasure within the finite limits of his physical organism; but man wants it to satisfy the infinite thirst of his soul. In man, therefore, the law of diminishing returns operates: As pleasure decreases, the desire for it increases. Pleasures then begin to exasperate because they "lie"; they do not give what they promised. Sadness, bitterness, and cynicism sometimes seize the soul, and with it a fatigue of life. That very emptiness can be the foundation of conversion. The desire for happiness could not be wrong. It must be, therefore, that we sought happiness in the wrong objects: in creatures apart from God, instead of in creatures under God's law. Thus, in the very confusion and disgust following sin is hidden a sense of awakened spiritual possibilities. A soul is on the verge of knowing itself when it knows that acting like a beast it *might* live like an angel. After having fed himself on husks, the prodigal began to yearn for the bread of the father's house.

There are various kinds of weariness: weariness of the body, which can be satisfied under any tree or even on a pillow of stone; weariness of the brain, which needs the incubation of rest for new thought to be born; but hardest of all to satisfy is weariness of heart, which can be healed only by communion with God.

In all other religions you have to be good to come to God. In Christianity, you do not. Christianity is realistic: it begins with the fact that, whatever you are, you are not what you *ought* to be. If everything in the world were perfectly good, we would still need God, for all goodness comes from God.

But the presence of evil makes that need more imperative. Christianity begins with the recognition that there is something in your life and in the world that *ought* not to be, that need not be, and that could be otherwise were it not for evil choices.

✠

May we never die too soon! This does not mean not dying young; it means not dying with our appointed tasks undone. It is indeed a curious fact that no one ever thinks of Our Lord as dying too young! That is because He finished His Father's business. But no matter how old we are when we die, we always feel there is something more to be done.

Why do we feel that way, if it is not because we did not do well the tasks assigned to us? Our task may not be great; it may be only to add one stone to the Temple of God. But whatever it is, do each tiny little act in union with your Savior who died on the Cross and you will *finish* your life. Then you will never die too young!

✠

There are two ways of coming to God: through the preservation of innocence; and through the loss of it. Some have come to God because they were good, like Mary, who was "full of grace" (Luke 1:28); like Joseph, the "just man" (Matt. 1:19); like Nathaniel, "in whom there was no guile" (see John 1:47); or like John the Baptist, "the greatest man ever born of woman" (see Matt. 11:11).

But others have come to God who were bad, like the young man of the Gerasenes "possessed with devils" (Matt. 8:28), like Magdalen, out of whose corrupt soul the Lord cast seven devils; and like the thief at the right who spoke the second word to the Cross.

✠

No character, regardless of the depths of its vice or its intemperance, is incapable of being transformed through the cooperation of Divine and human action into its opposite, of being lifted to the I-level and then to the Divine level.

Drunkards, alcoholics, dope fiends, materialists, sceptics, sensualists, gluttons, thieves—all can make that area of life in which they are defeated, the area of their greatest victory.

✠

Cease asking what God will give you if you come to Him, and begin to ask what you will give God. It is not the sacrifice it sounds, for, in having Him, you will have everything besides.

✠

In the face of that evil which is endemic in the human heart, this truth emerges: it is one thing to be blind and another thing to know it.

There is hope for those who are deaf and who want to hear and for the lame who want to walk, and there is hope for the diseased who acknowledges the need of a physician and the sinner who feels the need of a redeemer.

✠

The capacity for conversion is greater in the really wicked than in the self-satisfied and complacent. The very emptiness of soul of the sinners is in itself an occasion for receiving the compassion of God. Self-disgust is the beginning of conversion, for it marks the death of pride.

✠

We do recognize that with Protestants and Jews we have God, morality, and religion in common. In the name of God, let us, Jews, Protestants, and Catholics, do two things: (1) Realize that an attack upon one is an attack upon all, since we are all one in God; it is not Tolerance we need, but Charity; not forbearance but love.

(2) Begin doing something about religion, and the least we can do is to say our prayers: to implore God's blessings upon the world and our country; to thank Him for His blessings; and to become illumined in the fullness of His Truth.

25

What Death Is to the Body, Sin Is to the Soul

What death is to the body, that sin is to the soul. "For the wages of sin is death" (Rom. 6:23). Man in the state of grace has a double "life." The life of the body is the soul; the life of the soul is grace. When the soul leaves the body, the body dies. When grace leaves the soul, the soul dies.

Hatred is only love upside down.

Hate and love spring from the same passion, as laughter and sorrow drink from the same fountain of tears. The difference is in the motive and the end for which they live. Religion is something that must be either hated or loved. It cannot be watched!

Sloth is a malady of the will which causes neglect of one's duty. In the physical realm, it appears as laziness, softness, idleness, procrastination, nonchalance, and indifference; as a spiritual disease, it takes the forms of a distaste of the spiritual, lukewarmness at prayers, and contempt of self-discipline. Sloth is the sin of those who only look at picture magazines, but never at print; who read only novels, but never a philosophy of life. Sloth disguises itself as tolerance and broadmindedness—it has not enough intellectual energy to discover Truth and follow it. Sloth loves nothing, hates nothing, hopes nothing, fears nothing, keeps alive because it sees nothing to die for. It rusts out rather than wears out; it would not render a service to any employer a minute after a whistle blows; and the more it increases in our midst, the more burdens it throws upon the State. Sloth is egocentrical; it is basically an attempt to escape from social and spiritual responsibilities, in the expectation that someone else will care for us. The lazy man is a parasite. He demands that others cater to him and earn his bread for him; he is asking special privileges in wishing to eat bread which he has not earned.

Pride is an inordinate love of one's own excellence, either of body or mind, or the unlawful pleasure we derive from thinking we have no superiors.

Covetousness is an inordinate love of the things of this world. It becomes inordinate if one is not guided by a reasonable end, such as a suitable provision for one's family, or the future, or if one is too solicitous in amassing wealth, or too parsimonious in dispensing it.

The sin of covetousness includes therefore both the intention one has in acquiring the goods of this world and the manner of acquiring them. It is not the love of an excessive sum which makes it wrong, but an inordinate love of any sum.

Simply because a man has a great fortune, it does not follow that he is a covetous man. A child with a few pennies might possibly be more covetous. Material things are lawful and necessary in order to enable us to live according to our station in life, to mitigate suffering, to advance the Kingdom of God, and to save our souls.

Lust is an inordinate love of the pleasures of the flesh. The important word here is *inordinate* for it was Almighty God Himself who associated pleasure with the flesh. He attached pleasure to eating in order that we might not be remiss in nourishing and preserving our individual lives; He associated pleasure with the marital act in order that husband and wife might not be remiss in their social obligations to propagate mankind and raise children for the Kingdom of God.

The pleasure becomes sinful at that point where, instead of using it as a means, we begin to use it as an end. To eat for the sake of eating is a sin because eating is a means to an end, which is health. Lust, in like manner, is selfishness or perverted love.

✠

Anger is no sin under three conditions: (1) If the cause of anger be just, for example, defense of God's honor; (2) If it be no greater than the cause demands, that is, if it be kept under control; and (3) If it be quickly subdued: "Let not the sun go down upon your anger."

✠

Gluttony is an abuse of the lawful pleasure that God has attached to eating and drinking, which are a necessary means of self-preservation. It is an inordinate indulgence in the pleasures of eating and drinking, either by taking more than is necessary or by taking it at the wrong time or in too luxurious a manner. Gluttony disguises itself as "the good life," or as "the sophisticated way," or as "gracious living." An overstuffed, double-chinned generation takes gluttony for granted, rarely considering it a sin.

✠

Self-knowledge demands the discovery of our predominant fault—of the particular defect which tends to prevail in us, affecting our sympathies, our decisions, desires, and passions. The predominant fault is not always clearly seen, because it acts as a Fifth Column in our souls. A man who by nature is gentle and kind may easily have his spiritual life ruined by the hidden fault of weakness toward ethical and moral issues. Another person, who by nature is courageous, may have as his predominant fault a bad temper—or his fits of violence which he calls "courage." The existence of a predominant fault does not indicate that there is no good quality in us; yet our good qualities may possibly be rendered ineffective by this hidden defect. The quickest way to discover the predominant fault is to ask ourselves: What do I think about most when alone? Where do my thoughts go when I let them go spontaneously? What makes me most unhappy when I do not have it? Most glad when I possess it? What fault irritates me most when I am accused of it, and which sin do I most vigorously deny possessing?

✠

Anger is a violent desire to punish others.

✠

Unjust anger is a violent and inordinate desire to punish others, and is often accompanied by hatred which seeks not only to repel aggression, but to take revenge.

Am I impatient with others? Do I fly into "fits of temper" and make cutting and sarcastic remarks because my will has been crossed? Do I ever practice patience, that is, think before I speak, then talk to myself?

Have I ever asked myself how will God forgive my sins if I do not forgive the faults of others?

Do I realize that being quickly aroused to anger is a sign of selfishness, and that my character is known from the things I hate? If I love God, I will hate sin; if I love sin, I will hate religion. "Judge not, that you may not be judged" (Matt. 7:1).

✠

Envy is sadness at another's good, as if that good were an affront to one's superiority. As the rich are avaricious, so the poor are sometimes envious. The envious person hates to see anyone else happy. The charm, the beauty, the knowledge, the peace, the wealth of others are all regarded as having been purloined from him. Envy induces ugly women to make nasty remarks about beautiful women, and makes the stupid malign the wise. Since the envious person cannot go up, he tries to achieve equality by pulling the other down. Envy is always a snob, is always jealous and possessive. To the envious, all who are polite are castigated as "high-hat"; the religious they dub "hypocrites"; the well-bred "put on airs"; the learned are "high-brow." Envy begins by asking, "Why shouldn't I have everything that others have?" and ends by saying, "It is because others have these virtues that I do not have them." Then envy becomes enmity; it is devoid of respect and honor, and, above all, it can never say, "Thank you," to anyone.

✠

Envy is discontent with another's good, a mentality which is cast down at another's good, as if it were an affront to our own superiority.

Do I assert my envy by "running down" others by innuendo, half-truths, fault-finding, or by attributing to them false motives.

Have I rejoiced over the misfortunes of others?

Have I ever tried to cure my jealousy by praying for the one of whom I was jealous?

Why have I not made the quality of a neighbor an occasion for imitation rather than envy, and thus increased in some way the welfare of humanity and the glory of God: "But if you bite and devour one another: take heed you be not consumed one of another" (Gal. 5:15).

✠

There are some people who love to boast of their tolerance, but actually it is inspired by egotism; they want to be left alone in their own ideas, however wrong they be, so they plead for a tolerance of other people's ideas. But this kind of tolerance is very dangerous, for it becomes intolerance as soon as the ego is disturbed or menaced. That is why a civilization which is tolerant about false ideas instead of being charitable to persons is on the eve of a great wave of intolerance and persecution.

✠

Psychiatry is not as much a modern discovery as it is a modern need. Its method has been known for centuries, but there was never the occasion to apply it, because in other ages men knew they could not "get away with it." Their purgations, reparations, and amendments were settled on their knees in prayer, rather than on their back on a couch. But at that moment when the Divine and morality were denied, society came face to face with handling the mental effects which that very denial entailed. The crimes were not new, for people could snap their fingers just as much against the moral law in the days of faith as now. In those days when they did wrong, they lost the road, but they never threw away the map. But today when men do wrong they call it right. This creates, in addition to the moral problem which is denied, a mental problem. And that is where much psychiatry comes in. There is nothing new about the discovery that the reality we refuse to face we bury in our unconscious mind. What is new is the need to treat those who break the law and deny the law; who live by freedom and refuse to accept its consequences.

✠

Hatred comes from want of knowledge, as love comes from knowledge; thus, bigotry is properly related to ignorance.

The alarming amount of hatred loose in the modern world is largely caused by guilt; the man who hates himself soon begins to hate his fellow men.

✠

Hatred is hard to stop, for, if let alone, it sets off a chain reaction. One man's animosity arouses anger in another, who, in turn, creates rage in someone else. That is why our Lord told us when we are struck on one cheek, turn to the other: thus, by an interior effort of the will, we bring the chain of anger to an end. The only way to destroy hate is for an individual to absorb it and, in his own heart, convert it into love.

✠

There is a vast difference between the individual who gets drunk because he loves liquor and the one who does it because he hates or fears something else so much that he has to run away from it. The first becomes the drunkard, the second the alcoholic. The drunkard pursues the exhilaration of liquor; the alcoholic pursues the obliteration of memory. Very few women ever become alcoholics because they like alcohol; they become alcoholics because they violently dislike something else. That is why, in some instances, the cure of alcoholism implies the facing of the very problem one is seeking to escape. And this procedure is impossible without self-knowledge.

✠

Evil is always mutilation of the self. The man who overeats does not count on indigestion, but he gets it. The man who wills to steal has not aimed at prison, yet that is where he lands. When a traveler refuses to follow the guideposts showing him the right way, he may still, eventually, reach his goal by finding disappointment at the end of every false trail. Disorder is a stern teacher, and a slow one, but a certain one. The Spanish have a proverb: "He who spits against Heaven spits in his own face." Evil may triumph for a little while. It can win the first battle, but it loses the booty and the reward.

✠

Self-made rationalizations always justify the egotist's flight from Goodness—as St. Augustine said: "I want to be chaste, dear Lord, a little later on. Not now!"[36]

✠

Dissatisfaction sometimes can be the motive of true progress. Dissatisfied with the pen, man invented the printing press; dissatisfied with the chariot and the locomotive, he invented the airplane. There is implanted in everyone an impulse which drives the spirit to beat its wings like an imprisoned eagle in the cages of this earth until there is blood on its plumes. Did hearts but analyze this urge that is within them, which drives them away from the actual to the possible and makes them dig in the

[36] Augustine, *Confessions* 8, 7.

desert of their lives for new living springs, and climb every mountain to get a better look at Heaven, they would see that they are being drawn back again to God, from Whom they came.

✠

Avoiding the occasions of sin is the easiest way of avoiding sin itself. The way to keep out of trouble is to keep out of the situations that lead up to trouble. The alcoholic must avoid the first sip of the first drink; the libertine must keep away from pretty women; the evil-minded must flee the company of those who degrade him. Our Lord said, "He that loveth danger shall perish in it" (Sir. 3:27). Temptation is hard to overcome at the last moment, when the sin is within our reach; it is easy to overcome if we act decisively to avoid a situation in which we might be tempted. Environments can make sin repulsive or attractive to us, for our surroundings affect us all. But we can choose the environment we wish and can ruthlessly reject the one that leads to trouble. Our Lord told us, "If thy right eye scandalize thee, pluck it out and cast it from thee" (Matt. 5:29). This means that if the books we read, the homes we visit, the games we play cause us to stumble morally, then we should cut them out and cast them from us.

✠

Many a cross we bear is of our own manufacture; we made it by our sins. But the Cross which the Savior carried was not His, but ours. One beam in contradiction to another beam was the symbol of our will in contradiction to His own. To the pious women who met Him on the roadway, He said: "Weep not over me" (Luke 23:28). To shed tears for the dying Savior is to lament the remedy; it were wiser to lament the sin that caused it. If innocence itself took a Cross, then how shall we, who are guilty, complain against it.

✠

Two attitudes are possible in sin — two attitudes can be taken toward our lapses into sin: We can fall down, and get up; or we can fall down, and stay there.

✠

Everyone in the world is defeated in one area of life or another. Some fall away from their high ideals; others bemoan their failure to marry or, having married, lament because the state failed to realize all its hopes and promises; others experience a decline of virtue, a gradual slipping away into mediocrity, or a slavery to vice; others are subjected to weariness, a failure of health, or economic ruin. All these disappointments are voiced in the mournful regret: "If I only had my life to live over again!" But it is of the utmost importance that, in facing our defeats and failures, we shall never yield to discouragement; for discouragement, from a spiritual point of view, is the result of wounded self-love and is therefore a form of pride.

✠

Physical idleness deteriorates the mind; spiritual idleness deteriorates the heart. The joint action of air and water can turn a bar to rust. Therefore at every hour in the marketplace, man must ask himself: "Why stand I here idle?" (see Matt. 20:6).

✠

Those who live in sin hardly understand the horror of sin. The one peculiar and terrifying thing about sin is the more experience you have with it, the less you know about it. You become so identified with it that you know neither the depths to which you have sunk nor the heights from which you have fallen.

✠

Think not, that in order to "know life" you must "experience evil." Is a doctor wiser because he is prostrate with disease? Do we know cleanliness by living in sewers? Do we know education by experiencing stupidity? Do we know peace by fighting? Do we know the joys of vision by being blinded? Do you become a better pianist by hitting the wrong keys? You do not need to get drunk to know what drunkenness is.

The examination of conscience brings to the surface the hidden faults of the day; it seeks to discover the weeds that are choking the growth of God's grace and destroying peace of soul. It is concerned with thoughts, words, and deeds, with sins of omission and sins of commission. By omission, we mean the good that is left undone—a failure to aid a needy neighbor, a refusal to offer a word of consolation to those who are burdened with sorrow. Sins of commission involve malicious remarks, lies, acts of dishonesty, and those seven sins which are the seven pallbearers of the soul: self-love, inordinate love of money, illicit sex, hate, overindulgence, jealousy, and laziness. In addition to all this, there is the examination for what spiritual writers call our "predominant fault." Every person in the world has one sin which he commits more than others. Spiritual directors say that if we blotted out one great sin a year in a short time we should be perfect.

God is more anxious to save us than we are to save ourselves. There is a story told to the effect that one day Our Blessed Lord appeared to St. Jerome, saying to him, "Jerome, what will you give Me?" Jerome answered, "I will give you my writings," to which Our Lord replied that it was not enough. "Then," said Jerome, "what shall I give you? My life of penance and mortification?" But the answer was, "Even that is not enough!" "What have I left to give Thee?" cried Jerome. Our Blessed Lord answered, "Jerome, you can give Me your sins."

The atheist is properly defined as the person who has no invisible means of support.

Many people like to discuss religion, to argue about it, but as if it were impersonal, as if they were discussing Indonesian ritual dances. They miss the many splendored things because they never relate what they know to their own lives.

In every human being, there is a double law of gravitation, one pulling him to the earth, where he has his time of trial, and the other pulling him to God, where he has his happiness. The anxiety underlying all modern man's anxieties arises from his trying to be himself without God or from his trying to get beyond himself without God. The example of the mountain climber is not exact, for such a man has no helper on the upper peak to which he aspires. Man, however, has a helper—God on the upper peak of eternity reaches out His Omnipotent Hand to lift him up, even before man raises his voice in plea. It is evident that, even though we escaped all the anxieties of modern economic life, even though we avoided all the tensions which psychology finds in the unconsciousness and consciousness, we should still have that great basic fundamental anxiety born of our creatureliness. Anxiety stems fundamentally from irregulated desires, from the creature wanting something that is unnecessary for him or contrary to his nature or positively harmful to his soul. Anxiety increases in direct ratio and proportion as man departs from God. Every man in the world has an anxiety complex "because he has the capacity to be either saint or sinner."

So long as mercy is available for all who despair of their own confusion and conflicts and inner incompleteness, it follows that sin is never the worst thing that can happen to a man. The worst thing is the refusal to recognize his sins. For if we are sinners, there is a Savior. If there is a Savior, there is a Cross. If there is a Cross, there is a way of appropriating it to our lives, and our lives to it. When that is done, despair is driven out and we have the "peace which the world cannot give" (see John 14:27).

✠

Every law, physical or moral, has its penalties. If I disobey the law of health, nature penalizes me with sickness. If I disobey the moral law, I cannot eternally hope to escape its consequences as though I had not violated it.

✠

Suicide sometimes becomes the last resort to those who boast of an easy conscience; the disorder of a nature turned topsy-turvy—with the body subjugating the soul—seems no longer endurable. It is a psychological fact that a sense of something amiss within him makes a person strike his breast whenever he has done wrong. The faithful do it three times when they recite the words of the Confiteor, "through my fault, through my fault, through my most grievous fault." It is as if there were something evil inside us that we should like to beat and to subdue. The executioners on Calvary left the hill striking their breasts, as if to drive out their crime. When deep despair settles on a sinful soul which has no outlet—either because it denies God or because it refuses to have recourse to His Mercy—then this desire for self-infliction may reach a point where one takes his own life, as Judas did. The Judge has not yet appeared, and yet judgment had already judged: the elaborate and beautiful composite of body and soul was so disordered that the conscience now condemned it to be severed.

✠

The more a man exalts himself, the less God seems to him in comparison. The good man is never sure he is good because he measures himself by the Perfect; the evil man is quite sure he is good because he measures himself by himself.

✠

Agnosticism is an evil when it contends not only that an individual mind knows nothing, but also that no other mind knows anything. In this sense, it is cowardly, because it runs away from the problems of life. Only about 10 percent of the people think for themselves. Columnists and headline writers think for the greater percent of the remainder. Those who are left are the agnostics, who think agnosticism is an answer to the riddle of life. Agnosticism is not an answer. It is not even a question.

✠

The bitterest draught man can ever drink is the confession of his utter inadequacy. The world says that at this moment man is at his worst; actually, he is at his best. Man is at his worst if he falls into despair; but he is at his best if, humbled, he cries to God for help.

Acknowledgments

I want to thank Almighty God for the health of mind, body, and spirit to put together these reflections.

To my good wife, Isabel, my children, and my grandchildren, who keep me young at heart and are truly a blessing from God. Thank you for sharing in my joy.

I wish to express my gratitude to members of the Archbishop Fulton John Sheen Foundation in Peoria, Illinois—in particular, to the Most Rev. Daniel R. Jenky, C.S.C., Bishop of Peoria, for your leadership and fidelity to the cause of Sheen's canonization and the creation of this book.

To Julie Enzenberger, O.C.V., who repeated to me time and time again Sheen's words: "Believe the incredible, and you can do the impossible."[37]

To my good friend and radio mentor, Terry Barber. Your passion for bringing souls to Christ through the teachings of Archbishop Fulton J. Sheen is infectious. Your cassette tape ministry that began in the 1980's to help share the recordings and writings of Archbishop Fulton J. Sheen has enriched the lives of countless souls. Thank you for telling everyone who would listen, "Your life is worth living." Full Sheen ahead my friend! Full Sheen ahead!

[37] Fulton Sheen, *Through the Year with Fulton Sheen: Inspirational Readings for Each Day of the Year*, ed. Henry Dieterich (San Francisco: Ignatius Press, 2003), 205.

To the many seminarians, priests, religious, bishops, and cardinals I have met during this journey. Always remember the words of Archbishop Sheen that "The priest is not his own."

To the tens of thousands of people I have met in my travels, giving presentations about Archbishop Fulton J. Sheen at parishes, conferences, universities, high schools, church groups, and even pubs: thank you for sharing with me your many "Sheen Stories." I truly cherish each one of them.

And lastly, to Archbishop Fulton J. Sheen, whose teachings on prayer, the Sacraments, our Lord's Passion, and His Seven Last Words continue to inspire me to love God more and to appreciate the gift of the Church. His teachings and his encouragement to make a holy hour each day has been a true gift in my life. May I be so blessed as to imitate Archbishop Sheen's love for the saints, the Sacraments, the Eucharist, and for the Mother of God. May the good Lord grant him a very high place in Heaven!

—Al Smith

Fulton J. Sheen Works Used in This Book

1. *Love One Another*. New York: P.J. Kenedy & Sons, 1944.

2. *The Best of Fulton J. Sheen, God Love You*. New York: Maco Magazine Corp., 1955.
   Maco Magazine Corp. was granted permission to use passages from the following works in this publication:
   Religion without God. Longmans, Green & Co., 1928.
   The Life of All Living. New York: The Century Company, 1929.
   The Divine Romance. New York: The Century Company, 1930.
   Old Errors and New Labels. New York: The Century Company, 1931.
   Moods and Truths. New York: The Century Company, 1932.
   The Eternal Galilean. New York: D. Appleton-Century Company, 1934.
   Calvary and the Mass. New York: P.J. Kenedy & Sons, 1936.
   The Rainbow of Sorrow. New York: P.J. Kenedy & Sons, 1938.
   Victory Over Vice. New York: P.J. Kenedy & Sons, 1939.
   The Seven Virtues. New York: P.J. Kenedy & Sons, 1940.
   The Armor of God. New York: P.J. Kenedy & Sons, 1943.

Seven Words to the Cross. New York: P. J. Kenedy & Sons, 1944.

Love One Another. New York: P. J. Kenedy & Sons, 1944.

Seven Words of Jesus and Mary. New York: P. J. Kenedy & Sons, 1945.

Preface to Religion. New York: P. J. Kenedy & Sons, 1946.

Characters of the Passion. New York: P. J. Kenedy & Sons, 1947.

Communism and the Conscience of the West. Indianapolis: Bobbs-Merrill Company, 1948.

Way to Happiness. New York: George Matthew Adams Service, 1949.

Peace of Soul. New York: McGraw-Hill, 1949.

Lift Up Your Heart. New York: McGraw-Hill, 1950.

Way to Inner Peace. New York: George Matthew Adams Service, 1950.

Three to Get Married. New York: Appleton-Century-Crofts, 1951.

The World's First Love. New York: McGraw Hill, 1952.

About the Author

Fulton John Sheen was born in El Paso, Illinois, in 1895. In high school, he won a three-year university scholarship, but he turned it down to pursue a vocation to the priesthood. He attended St. Viator College Seminary in Illinois and St. Paul Seminary in Minnesota. In 1919, he was ordained a priest for the Diocese of Peoria, Illinois. He earned a licentiate in sacred theology and a bachelor of canon law at the Catholic University of America and a doctorate at the Catholic University of Louvain, Belgium.

Sheen received numerous teaching offers but declined them in obedience to his bishop and became an assistant pastor in a rural parish. Having thus tested his obedience, the bishop later permitted him to teach at the Catholic University of America and at St. Edmund's College in Ware, England, where he met G. K. Chesterton, whose weekly BBC radio broadcast inspired Sheen's later NBC broadcast, *The Catholic Hour* (1930–1952).

In 1952, Sheen began appearing on ABC in his own series; *Life Is Worth Living*. Despite being given a time slot that forced him to compete with Milton Berle and Frank Sinatra, the dynamic Sheen enjoyed enormous success and in 1954 reach tens of millions of viewers, non-Catholics as well as Catholics.

When asked by Pope Pius XII how many converts he had made, Sheen responded, "Your Holiness, I have never counted them. I am always afraid if I did count them, I might think I made them, instead of the Lord."[38]

Sheen gave annual Good Friday homilies at New York's St. Patrick's Cathedral, led numerous retreats for priests and religious, and preached at summer conferences in England.

"If you want people to stay as they are," he said, "tell them what they want to hear. If you want to improve them, you tell them what they should know."[39] This he did, not only in his preaching but also in the more than ninety books he wrote. His *Peace of Soul* was sixth on the *New York Times* bestseller list.

Sheen served as auxiliary bishop of New York (1951–1966) and as bishop of Rochester (1966–1969).

Two of his great loves were for the Blessed Mother and the Eucharist. He made a daily holy hour before the Blessed Sacrament, from which he drew strength and inspiration to preach the gospel and in the presence of which he prepared his homilies. "I beg [Christ] every day to keep me strong physically and alert mentally in order to preach His gospel and proclaim His Cross and Resurrection," he said. "I am so happy doing this that I sometimes feel that when I come to the good Lord in Heaven, I will take a few days' rest and then ask Him to allow me to come back again to this earth to do some more work."

Sheen also said that "the greatest love story of all time is contained in a tiny white Host."[40] This was the love that transformed him. His daily eucharistic holy hour was legendary. From the day of his ordination to the day of his death, Sheen spent an hour a day praying in the presence of the Blessed Sacrament. From his office desk, through an open door,

[38] "May 8, 1895: The Birthday of Archbishop Fulton J. Sheen," Papal Artifacts, May 7, 2021, https://www.papalartifacts.com/may-8-1895-birthday-archbishop-fulton-j-sheen/.

[39] Fr. Daniel P. Noonan, *The Passion of Fulton Sheen* (New York: Dodd, Mead, & Company, 1972), 60.

[40] Sheila J. Nayar, *Dante's Sacred Poem: Flesh and the Centrality of the Eucharist to the* Divine Comedy (New York: Bloomsbury, 2014), 210.

he could gaze upon the tabernacle at all times. His union with Christ enabled him to more fully, more accurately, and more convincingly lead others to Christ in all he said and did. Sheen was a man of many talents and accomplishments, but it was Christ who enabled him to use them in the best ways.

The good Lord called Fulton Sheen home in 1979. His television broadcasts, now on tape, and his books continue his earthly work of winning souls for Christ. Sheen's cause for canonization was opened in 2002. In 2012, Pope Benedict XVI declared him "Venerable." In 2019, Pope Francis approved a miracle attributed to the intercession of the Venerable Fulton Sheen, clearing the way for his beatification.

Sophia Institute

Sophia Institute is a nonprofit institution that seeks to nurture the spiritual, moral, and cultural life of souls and to spread the Gospel of Christ in conformity with the authentic teachings of the Roman Catholic Church.

Sophia Institute Press fulfills this mission by offering translations, reprints, and new publications that afford readers a rich source of the enduring wisdom of mankind.

Sophia Institute also operates the popular online resource CatholicExchange.com. *Catholic Exchange* provides world news from a Catholic perspective as well as daily devotionals and articles that will help readers to grow in holiness and live a life consistent with the teachings of the Church.

In 2013, Sophia Institute launched Sophia Institute for Teachers to renew and rebuild Catholic culture through service to Catholic education. With the goal of nurturing the spiritual, moral, and cultural life of souls, and an abiding respect for the role and work of teachers, we strive to provide materials and programs that are at once enlightening to the mind and ennobling to the heart; faithful and complete, as well as useful and practical.

Sophia Institute gratefully recognizes the Solidarity Association for preserving and encouraging the growth of our apostolate over the course of many years. Without their generous and timely support, this book would not be in your hands.

www.SophiaInstitute.com
www.CatholicExchange.com
www.SophiaInstituteforTeachers.org